KIOWA·VOICES

Saynday, the Kiowa culture hero, wandered alone on the sunless earth until he discovered the Kiowas living underground. He enabled the people, as ants, to crawl upward through a hollow cottonwood tree and pulled them through a Sawpole's (owl's) hole upon the darkened face of the earth.

KIOWA·VOICES

KIOWA·VOICES

KIOWA·VOICES

CEREMONIAL DANCE, RITUAL AND SONG

VOLUME I

BY MAURICE BOYD

LINN PAUAHTY, KIOWA CONSULTANT

THE KIOWA HISTORICAL AND RESEARCH SOCIETY, CONSULTANTS

DONALD E. WORCESTER, ASSOCIATE EDITOR

THE TEXAS CHRISTIAN UNIVERSITY PRESS
FORT WORTH, TEXAS 76129

THIRD PRINTING
Copyright © 1981 by The Texas Christian University Press

Library of Congress Catalog Card No. 81-50977
Manufactured in the United States of America

ISBN 0-912646-67-5

To all great story tellers

and those who enjoy listening

Frontispiece: Peyote Visions by Robert Redbird. During the Peyote ceremony, lasting from sundown until sunrise, the Peyote Priest's rattle and the hypnotic waving of the peyote fan amidst the spiraling smoke produces a stimulating effect upon those who participate in the ceremony. The four peyote buttons at the upper left represent the minimum required amount of sacramental food to be eaten by each participant throughout the evening. The large peyote button at the bottom, called Father Peyote, rests on the evergreen sage which represents eternal life. The stalk of corn represents the regenerative power of the Earth-maker, the Great Mystery. The moon is a great power-carrier supplying some of the universal regenerative force. The cormorant bird represents the messenger power carrying the prayers from those on earth to the Great Powers beyond. The twelve eagle feathers plus the one worn by the Peyote Priest equals the thirteen eagle feathers found in an eagle's tail. The eagle-feather fan held by the priest contains the eagle power and suggests the freedom and power symbolized by the eagle.   Permission of Helen and James McCorpin.

Contents

Illustrations

Maps

Preface

FOR GENERATIONS THE KIOWAS HAVE CAREFULLY and lovingly passed along their tribal memory from parents to children. This remarkable Kiowa memory chain, which has linked the people to their past, is now in danger of being broken. The elderly preservers of oral history and tradition are dying out. A tribal memory chain, once broken, is beyond repair.

Faced with this danger of losing their cultural heritage, the source of their dignity and pride, many tribal elders have realized the need to record permanently their folk memory. They are eager to reveal the relationships between Kiowa cultural beliefs and values, dance and song, art and folklore. They also recognize the need to present historical events so that tribal actions may be viewed and evaluated against the tapestry of Kiowa culture rather than against an inappropriate European cultural background.

These views were most aptly expressed by James Twohatchett, a Kiowa of Hobart, Oklahoma, at the 1974 American Indian Festival in Anadarko:

> *How would you like for strangers to dig up the remains of your grandparents or parents in the name of scholarship? Or after spending a short time here, write a book about our people and folklore and pose as Kiowa experts with their "analysis" of us? You would not appreciate it if an outsider did this in your home, and neither do we. These culturally insensitive people, despite their good intentions, are not the ones who should tell our story.*

The growing concern prompted two Kiowa elders, James Auchiah and Linn Pauahty, to propose this project to this writer through their friend and tribal blood brother, George Younkin, then Archival Director of the Federal Records and National Archives Center, Fort Worth, Texas. The need for action was imperative. Enlisting the support of Texas Christian University, this writer collaborated with the Kiowas on the project.

The Kiowa Tribal Council approved the project in 1975 and organized the Kiowa Historical and Research Society, which was incorporated by the State of Oklahoma. With research grants from the National Endowment for the Arts and from Texas Christian University, the Society made contact with tribal elders who recorded and translated their oral history, which was then transcribed, edited, and resubmitted to the Society for accuracy. Many Kiowa families also supplied valuable source materials, including priceless tribal calendars, ancient Kiowa artifacts, nineteenth-century photographs, native paintings and drawings, and recordings of Kiowa music, dances, and songs.

Relying upon a folk memory that extends backward over two hundred years, the Kiowas have checked tribal knowledge against the accounts of ethnologists, linguists, historians, and observers before approving their final account. Where tribal knowledge disagrees with other accounts, the Kiowas have given their version in this study. Five Kiowa "winter counts" or calendars recording principal tribal events since 1832 in pictographs have been consulted to check or corroborate verbal accounts.

This first of three volumes of *Kiowa Voices*, therefore, represents part of the tribal effort to preserve their history and culture. With additional funds from the National Endowment for the Humanities and the Texas Christian University Press, publication of these materials was assured. The volumes present Kiowa ceremonial dances and ritual, songs and music, myths and legends, art and folklore.

I am indebted to many individuals and institutions. Without Linn Pauahty and the Kiowa Historical and Research Society, the work would neither have been started nor completed. I wish to thank tribal members who donated time and material: James Auchiah, Edna Hokeah Pauahty, Jacob Ahtone, Ioleta Hunt McElheney Tiger, Luke Toyebo, Parker and Jeanette Brace, Yale and Mary Taneqoot (Spottedbird), Mark Sadongei, Gertrude Hines, Laura White Horse, Margaret Tsoodle, Gina Quoe-tone Pauahty, Juanita Cortez, Lee Satepetaw, David and Emma Apekaume, Nina Kodaseet, David Poolaw, James Twohatchett, Sally Bointy, Ernest Hunt, and Sallie Kaulaity. That some of the contributors have not lived to see their efforts in print underscores the urgency.

For their kindness in making available the manuscript collection of Susan Peters — the accumulation of fifty years of oral history and other materials by the now deceased Kiowa field matron — I wish to thank Mrs. Helen McCorpin and Mrs. Jane Pattie. They organized and assisted with the editing of the material in Volume II derived from the Susan Peters papers.

Charley Redbird and Linn Pauahty assisted with the "new form" of Kiowa spelling used in the volumes. Their recent studies on the Kiowa language have proved most helpful. Scott Tonemah and his wife permitted photographic use of their collection of Kiowa arts and crafts and supplied valuable information about Monroe Tsatoke, Kiowa art, and peyotism.

The taped collection of Indian music by Linn Pauahty is one of the largest private collections of Native American music in existence. A lifetime collector of Kiowa dance and music, Pauahty made available his tapes and knowledge of Kiowa dance and song for this work. George Tahbone, a Kiowa dancer, also contributed information, and his wife

Linn Pauahty, son of one of the last Buffalo Medicine Cult members, is the keeper of one of the original Buffalo Medicine Cult bags dating from 1822. The pipe he holds has the original bowl smoked at the Medicine Lodge Treaty of 1867.
Photo courtesy Kiowa Historical and Research Society (KHRS).

James Auchiah, a grandson of the Kiowa chief Satanta and one of the famous "Kiowa Five" artists, wears the ceremonial regalia of his famous ancestor on the occasion when Satanta's body was reburied at Fort Sill cemetery in 1963. Courtesy KHRS.

Marjie Queton translated two Saynday stories orally rendered by her mother, Eilene Bointy Queton. The Palmer family supplied pictures of George and Dixon Palmer in both traditional and fancy dance costumes.

A descendant of Chief Big Tree and the present keeper of his calendar provided an oral interview concerning the calendar, a partial copy of which was in Mrs. Peters' collection. And through the efforts of Gina and Linn Pauahty, the Keah-ko calendar was also located. Its keeper, Lawrence Ware, consented to our use of its summer and winter pictographs covering the years from 1860 to 1887.

Mrs. Carole Frame made available the papers of her father, Robert Onco, the son of Anko, the nineteenth-century Kiowa calendar man. They contained valuable insights into Kiowa culture and symbols; fifteen Saynday stories, including Mrs. Frame's paintings of Saynday, were also among the papers. In addition, she translated some legendary material orally rendered by Eva Satepahoodle.

Several professional Kiowa artists gave generously of their time and talent. For Volume I, Roland Whitehorse provided the Kiowa tribal logo in addition to twelve illustrations for the Rabbit society and Kiowa children at play. C. E. Rowell, the grandson of Sun Boy, kindly drew thirty illustrations and a painting of Kiowa life before reservation days. Mr. and Mrs. James McCorpin made available their collection of works by Kiowa artists Robert Redbird and Lee Tsatoke. Use of Kevin Tonip's peyote painting was by permission of Jon Christopher Boyd.

For Volume II, Bobby Hill (White Buffalo) supplied thirty illustrations for the legends. Barthell Littlechief created the color painting and forty illustrations for the Saynday stories. Sharron Ahtone Harjo, the former Miss Kiowa and Miss Indian America of 1965, has been represented by one of her Saynday paintings from this author's collection. Also from the same collection are the river monster and two nineteenth-century Saynday paintings by Hagoon (Silverhorn) and the Spirit Horse by Woody Crumbo, not a Kiowa but an associate of the original "Five Kiowa" artists. Two long-time Kiowa enthusiasts supplied needed supplemental sketches: Richard W. Pemberton for the legends and Thomas W. Boyd for the calendars. James Auchiah, who died before completing his illustrations for this work, left valuable accounts and some "verbal pictures" through oral interviews during the last months of his life.

The University of Oklahoma Library staff proved invaluable; my special thanks go to Dr. Arrell M. Gibson, head of the Division of Manuscripts, and Mr. Jack D. Haley, archivist. Mr. Sam Olkinetsky, director of the Museum of Art of the University of Oklahoma, provided paintings selected from the Five Kiowa artists and Lois Smoky. Mr. Arthur Silberman, the Oklahoma City critic of Indian painting, offered invaluable suggestions. Mr. Gillett Griswold, former director of the Fort Sill Museum, and his staff were courteous and untiring in their aid.

Other institutions permitting use of their works are the Museum of the American Indian, Heye Foundation, New York City; the Department of Anthropology, Smithsonian Institution, Washington, D.C.; the Phil-brook Art Center, Tulsa, Oklahoma; the National Archives, Washington, D.C.; the Amon Carter Museum of Western Art, Fort Worth, Texas; the Oklahoma Historical Society, Indian Archives, Oklahoma City, Okla-homa; the Office of Indian Affairs, Department of the Interior, Washington, D.C.; the Museum of the Great Plains, Lawton, Oklahoma; the Southern Plains Indian Museum and Craft Shop, Anadarko, Oklahoma.

My deepest appreciation for sharing family photographic treasures goes to Gladys Komalty Davenport, granddaughter of Chief Komalty; Evelyn Horse Bread, granddaughter of Chief Hunting Horse; and Hen-rietta Tongkeamah.

The Mary Couts Burnett Library staff of Texas Christian University assisted the project in dozens of ways, directly and indirectly; special thanks must go to Dr. Paul Parham and Miss Mary Charlotte Faris for their forebearance with me. Mrs. Goldie West of the Fort Worth Inde-pendent Public School District drew upon her editorial skills and Native American background to offer innumerable suggestions.

The visual appeal of this volume is the result of the personal interest and esthetic talents of Judy Oelfke Smith, who sensitively plied her art in the graphic design and production of this book. She has set the leg-ends apart from the text with the use of large type, in hopes that they might be easily found and enjoyed by young Kiowas. Also, the volume has been designed for use as a reference book, though care has been taken to maintain visual appeal for effective display of Kiowa art. We cannot thank her enough for the sense of balance and harmony she has given this volume.

Even with the support of the above people and institutions, only the sustaining guidance and editorial assistance of Linn Pauahty and Dr. Donald E. Worcester, my colleague of twenty-five years, enabled me to complete the project.

Maurice Boyd

| INTRODUCTION

1 Kiowa Legendary Origins

We Kiowa are old, but we dance.
  Ageless. Our dance is spirited.
Today's twisting path is temporary;
  the path will be gone tomorrow,
  but the folk memory remains.
Our forefathers' deeds touch us,
  shape us, like strokes of a painting.
  In endless procession, their deeds mark us.
The elders speak knowingly of forever.

                    —James Auchiah[1]

Saynday Finds His People

THE SMALL KIOWA TRIBE was bound together in its legendary beginnings, when the earth was empty of people. Saynday, the Kiowa culture hero, wandered alone on the sunless earth until he discovered the Kiowas living underground. He enabled the people, as ants, to crawl upward through a hollow cottonwood tree and pulled them through a Saw-pole's (owl's) hole upon the darkened face of the earth. More would have come out, but a pregnant female became stuck in the hole and blocked the way. And so only a few sprang forth fresh with hope, determined to survive.[2]

TODAY THIS TRADITION IS JOYOUSLY EXPRESSED by a modern Kiowa poet: "Behold! I am alive, I am alive!"[3] The people first called themselves *Kwu'-da* (pulling out) and *Tép-dá* (coming out). Much later the Comanches called them Kaigwa, a word without meaning in the Kiowa language, but culturally interpreted as "Principal People."[4]

The white man's scholars say the remote ancestors of the Kiowas crossed from Siberia over the frozen tundra to Alaska. Most of them declare there were two great migrations between 25,000 and 8,000 B.C., the latest being that of the Eskimo-Aleut-Athapaskans. Of these things tribal memory recalls nothing, although some scholars have attempted to link them with the Athapaskans.

For at least 10,000 years the migratory peoples of the Western Hemisphere evolved completely apart from other races elsewhere in the world. They developed reddish bronze skin that can withstand the sun and jet black hair that resists turning gray in old age if the "Indian" is full-blooded. Other unique physical characteristics include little or no facial or body hair, broad cheek bones, and shovel-shaped incisor teeth with lateral ridges.[5]

Throughout the millenia these Native Americans also developed customs and beliefs which they wove into a total way of life. This separate cultural development, completely unrelated to the cultures evolving in Europe, Africa, and Asia, produced a people with unique psychological traits.

The centuries of independent physical and cultural development created among the American Indians the special "Indian sensibility" mentioned by Jamake Highwater, a Blackfoot/Cherokee, and reaffirmed by T. C. Cannon, Kiowa/Caddo.[6] Scott Momaday, the gifted Kiowa poet and Pulitzer Prize winner, calls it a "blood recollection," a synthesis of "the tribal intelligence, an exposition of racial memory."[7] But whether genetic or cultural, the Kiowa tribe is acutely aware of its "Indianness." The individual Kiowa also knows that he cannot sever himself from the living tribal entity any more than he can dissociate himself from the sustaining earth or the psychological support of the spirit forces of the universe.

Linguistic scholars of other races suggest that the early migrants brought from Asia to the Americas six basic languages, or possibly a few more. From these foundation languages approximately three hundred variations and dialects emerged, all spoken by the numerous tribes when white people came centuries later. Most theorists maintain the Kiowa language is an offshoot of the Azteco-Tanoan group. Many Kiowas, however, believe their language stands alone and unique.[8]

Through oral communication and folk memory, the Kiowas preserved their tribal history. Not until 1832 by the Christian calendar did they use pictographs in their "winter counts" or calendars to record the significant tribal events of each year.

Oral tradition says that Saynday provided his people with the sun and its power. They then beheld the earthly wonders of *Dom-oye-alm-daw-k'hee,** the Earth-maker, and marveled at the wooded hills and the wild game, the streams winding through the valleys, the ripened berries on the edge of the prairies, and the leaping fish breaking the lakes' surfaces.

The Kiowas shared the land in common, subsisting on nature's bounty. Individual ownership of land was inconceivable, for the soil

*Sometimes referred to as Doyem Daw-
  k'hee in the old spelling.

Winter 1832-33 (Dohasan Calendar). *Black Wolf was killed and the Kiowas captured a large quantity of silver coins in an encounter in the Texas Panhandle*

Winter 1865-66 (Keah-ko Calendar). *Chief Dohasan, the originator of the oldest Kiowa calendar that has been preserved, died this winter.*

Saynday and his Friends. *A nineteenth-*
century Kiowa painting on doeskin.
Courtesy Smithsonian Institution.

Indian Sensibility—In Good Relation to the Spirit Powers *by Robert Redbird. Courtesy James and Helen McCorpin.*

Owl and Medicine Man *by C. E. Rowell (1976). The owl was the symbol of wisdom, and Kiowas believed it could prophesy. Medicine men called to the owl and talked with it in times of danger or trouble, and relayed its prophesies to the tribe. The owl was feared, for its repeated hoot was the omen of death. Courtesy a private collection.*

was part of the Earth-maker's handiwork to be enjoyed by all. The feeling of oneness with the universe and created things—the earth and all living creatures, including themselves—early became a tribal psychological characteristic. Saynday spoke in a language understood by animals and by people. No distinction existed between the Kiowas, who had emerged as ants from the cottonwood tree, and other living creatures. All were part of nature's whole, part of *the Earth-maker's* creation. When a Kiowa says "Behold! I stand in good relation to the earth and its creatures," he reflects his feeling of oneness with the universe.[9]

Throughout the centuries the Kiowas witnessed floods and volcanic eruptions, and they marveled at the power of *Dom-oye-alm-daw-k'hee* as the Recreator of the Earth. They felt the force of the four winds and respected the Earth-maker's mysterious spirit power, *Daw-k'hee.* Amidst these wonders, they prayed to the spirit god reflected through the sun, *Pahy-ghya-daw-kee.* The Kiowas accepted creation as good and they lived as free people in the natural order. The deer and the fox, prairie dog and coyote were all fellow creatures possessing souls, even as the ants who crawled from the cottonwood tree to become the Kiowas.[10]

Some animals, however, apparently embodied more of the natural force than others. The Kiowas regarded the bear as a powerful but sinister force. The owl, representing power and death, was associated with the Doyem-k'hee or tribal healers whom the white men called "Medicine Men." The word "medicine" to the Kiowas means "spirit power" or "mystery," not a medicinal drug. The medicine men could, through concentrated effort and meditative discipline, gain contact with the invisible spiritual forces of the universe.[11]

The original creative power of the universe, called Dom-oye-alm-daw-k'hee (magic, or super-power, earth-maker god) by Kiowas and the Great Spirit by white men, was a force not directly associated with all human affairs. Some of the tribe in early times believed that the lesser gods or "powers" involved in primeval creation eventually had grown old and died long ago. The following song suggests this tribal idea.

> This song is reminding you
> that all things will come to an end;
> Even our gods will end,
> sometime, somewhere.
> —*Old Kiowa Song*[12]

If the song expresses a truth, then the power of former gods associated with the original creative spirit survives only in their living creations. During their dances and songs the Kiowas as individuals feel the total tribal power, the tribal spiritual force, merge with the universal power. Then each Kiowa can affirm: "Behold! I stand in good relation to the spirit powers!"[13]

2 The Tribal Spirit Force

They carried dreams in their voices;
They were the elders, the old ones.
They told us the old stories,
And they sang the spirit songs.

—Big Tree[14]

NO ONE REMEMBERS WHEN THE KIOWAS first learned to use fire, roast meat, work stone, or paint with red oxide. The Kiowas say that Saynday taught them these things long ago. He also enabled them to survive the age of primordial mountain monsters.

The chain of tribal memory goes back only to the time when they used dog travois in northern lands. The travois was an A-frame made of lodge poles attached to a dog's shoulders. Dogs could pull thirty-five to seventy-five pounds on a travois, depending on the size and health of the animal. Women bore the responsibility of making the lodge, or tipi, and moving it to a new camp. The lodgepole made from a special pine was the women's choice because it had a nearly uniform diameter throughout its length.[15]

The Kiowas relate to the land of the Canadian Rockies and to the Sarsi tribe on the headwaters of the northern Saskatchewan. Whether the Kiowas once lived in the region or merely hunted there is not known, but they did intermarry with the Sarsis. Chiefs of later years, Satank and Ga'apiatan, had some Sarsi blood.

The Kiowa hunting grounds in early times were limited in extent because travel by foot was difficult and slow. Hunting was often a group effort, for only in this way could they secure enough meat for all. A few hunters went upwind and chased the animals into a corral formed by the rest of the tribe. If a cliff or closed canyon were nearby, they drove the antelope or buffalo over the cliff or into the canyon, killing as many as they could. The hunters used heavy lances and tall bows with long arrows for distance shooting. In warfare large shields three feet in diameter were also employed.

Tribal memory places this style of nomadic life in the territory of western Montana around Indian (Virginia) City. The earliest known Kiowa hunting grounds were between the headwaters of the Yellowstone and the *P'haw-ayle*, or Big River (Missouri).[16]

Associated with the Kiowas during or before the Yellowstone River days were a band known as the Kiowa-Apaches. Neither Kiowa nor Apache, the Kiowa-Apaches were a band of Athapaskans distantly related to the Sarsis, and they called themselves "Nadi-isha-Dena" or "principal people." Although they were a part of the Kiowa movement, their language was unlike the Kiowas' and their band always camped separately.

THE KIOWA AND THE GREAT PLAINS, 1200-1600

Adapted from Francis Haines, The Plains Indians: Their Origins, Migrations, and Cultural Development *(New York, 1976).*

Kiowa Pre-horse Culture Dress *of Yellowstone era. Pictured is Old-Man Silverhorn (Ha-goon), son of Daun-pi (Donpay) or Shoulder Blade, at the Craterville Indian Fair, Cache, Oklahoma, 1926.*
Courtesy KHRS.

The Half-boy Legend

The tribal elders know that long ago, during the summer months in the Yellowstone, the Kiowas and the Kiowa-Apaches held a dance of thanksgiving to *Zye-da Tah'-lee*, the supernatural half-boy who was known as the son of the Sun. The following legend explains why the Kiowas revere Tah'-lee.

A MAN AND HIS WIFE CAREFULLY watched after their little girl. But one day they left her with a friend who placed the cradled child in a tree. A beautiful yellow bird* gently settled on the limb next to her. The child crawled from the cradle and climbed after the bird, which ascended higher and higher in the tree. Then the tree itself grew taller, and the child and bird were lifted into the sky. Suddenly they were in a strange place. The girl was now a woman and the bird was a young man, the Sun.

Eventually the woman had a child, the son of the Sun. She was lonely in the strange place and desired to return to her people. She dared to uproot a special bush cropped by a buffalo which the Sun had forbidden her to touch. A hole appeared where the roots of the plant had been, and she saw her people far below on earth. Dropping a rope through the hole, she climbed down with her child. Unfortunately the rope extended only half way to earth. When the Sun came home that evening and saw her on the end of the rope, he angrily threw a ring (a gaming wheel) and it struck her dead.

The boy survived on earth, and he lived for a long time with a grandmother spider. One day he threw the ring into the air. It came down and struck him on the head, cutting him in half. Now there were two boys, half-boys, for the grandmother to care for. Years passed, the grandmother spider died, and the two boys sur-

Some Kiowa versions call it a porcupine, others a redbird.

vived many escapades.

Eventually one of the boys walked into the waters of Spear Lake in Wyoming and disappeared forever. The remaining boy transformed himself into ten portions of medicine, the ten sacred medicine bundles of the Kiowas. In this way Tah'-lee, the half-boy or boy-God, gave himself as an offering to the Kiowas.[17]

THE SPIRIT POWER OF THE SON OF THE SUN remains today in the bundles. When the Kiowas pray before the bundles, they are not praying directly to the medicine bags; they are praying to Tah'-lee, whose canonized memory is invoked when the Kiowas contemplate the medicine bags and their spirit power derived from Tah'-lee.

The word "Tah'-lee," pronounced Tah'-lhee and meaning "boy," contains the idea of "boy-God" to the Kiowas. A clarification is necessary concerning the misuse of the term "ten grandmothers" to refer to the ten medicine bundles bearing the spirit power of Tah'-lee.

"Taw-lee" is the Kiowa word for "paternal grandmother" and has been confused with "Tah'-lee," or half-boy. When the Kiowas refer to the ten sacred medicine bundles of their tribe, they mean the ten bundles containing the spirit force of Tah'-lee, and not ten grandmothers. The error arose in white people's writings because of the similarity between the accented Tah'-lee (half-boy) and the unaccented Taw-lee (paternal grandmother).

Another misconception persists in relation to the term "half-boys." Outsiders have incorrectly called the two boys "twin-boys." In the legend, when the son of the Sun threw the ring (wheel) into the air, he was split into two parts as the ring fell on his head. The resulting two boys, known to the Kiowas only as "half-boys," represented two halves of the original son of the Sun, the mortal and immortal halves. The mortal half-boy disappeared in Lake Spear; the immortal half-boy remains today as the spirit force in the ten medicine bundles.

The erroneous term "twin-boys" implies equal or similar substance. Obviously the two half-boys were not of the same essence or substance.[18]

KIOWA MIGRATORY RANGE, ca. 1680-1820

3 The Kiowa Saga: Horse-Buffalo Culture and Sun Dance

Our ancestors participated in a saga,
  a great migration of long ago.
The spirit horse carried triumphant braves
  to a rendezvous with spirit forces.
The buffalo power cared for our people's needs.
                              —Linn Pauahty[19]

THE KIOWA SAGA BEGAN LONG AGO IN THE north country. In the land of the Yellowstone the Kiowas felt great personal power. They had faced the sun, learned the trails, and conquered the mountains. After many years, however, they became restless in the Yellowstone vastness.

Westward and north the panoramic sweep revealed ranges of mountains stretching against the horizon in shades of green, brown, purple, and misty blues. In that direction the past tribal experience was compatible with the demands of the earth and their friends—the Flatheads.

Eastward and south lay vast unknown prairies and unfriendly tribes, but also millions of life-sustaining buffalo. Though legend recounts that some Kiowas chose the northwest route, the bulk of the tribe turned east and southward for what proved to be their great trek through the land of seemingly limitless prairies abundant with buffalo.

A well-known Kiowa legend explains why most of the tribe left for the plains.

The "Pulling-out" Band Legend

LONG AGO TWO CHIEFS LED a Kiowa hunting party in the land of the Yellowstone* in the north. After a long search they finally discovered an antelope and gave chase. One of the leaders of the party sent an arrow through the animal's heart and the hunt ended. Almost immediately an argument arose between two chiefs over possession of the udder of the slain antelope. The chief who killed the animal finally received the prized udder, considered a delicacy with strong "medicine," but the tribe split permanently into two factions. The losing chief angrily took his followers

*Another version places the setting nearer the Black Hills.

northwestward and disappeared from history. To this day the Kiowas do not know for certain what happened to the Kuáto or "Pulling Out" band. Possibly the group was wiped out in an ambush by the Dakotas (Sioux). The victorious chief took the main body of Kiowas southeastward toward the Black Hill country.[20]

THE KIOWAS LEFT THE MONTANA HIGH COUNTRY of the Yellowstone after 1682, for by that time they had acquired horses. From the headwaters of the Yellowstone they journeyed eastward across northern Wyoming by way of the Devil's Tower into the Black Hills of South Dakota.

The Bear Lodge (Devil's Tower) legend symbolically demonstrates how the spirit force protected the Kiowas on their journey. The story explains how seven sisters, the Star Girls, possibly representing the seven Kiowa bands existing at that time, escaped from a great bear which represented the threat of annihilation.

ONCE LONG AGO SEVERAL KIOWA girls were taking turns at imitating a bear and chasing the others. One girl, whose family lived under a bear taboo, reluctantly agreed to play the bear after she warned her sister to flee at the first sign of danger. Then suddenly something took possession of the bear girl's spirit. She shook all over and dropped to her hands and feet. As she chased the girls on all fours, her hands and feet grew claws and her body sprouted fur; a bear had replaced the girl. It chased, caught, and devoured the others while the sister escaped down a trail where she encountered six other Kiowas.* As the bear approached, they fled terrified over hills and across rivers. Finally the girls came to a stone,** and it

Moving Camp *by Stephen Mopope. The horse travois of the nineteenth century is depicted.*
Courtesy U.S. Department of the Interior.

The Bear Lodge Legend

*Another version says the fleeing sister met six Kiowa boys. A Sioux legend says boys were involved.
**Some versions say the girls came to a tree trunk.

spoke to them. It told them to climb on it, and as they did so it rapidly grew to an enormous height in the sky. The bear raced up to kill them, but the girls were beyond its reach. The animal tried four times to leap up to the pinnacle of the rock; each time it left deep claw marks which are still visible today on the face of the rock. Eventually the seven girls were safely lifted into the sky, where they remain today as the seven stars of the Big Dipper.[21]

THE KIOWAS STRESS THE CREATIVE POWER of Dom-oye-alm-daw-k'hee, the Earth-maker who used his power to protect the Kiowas from the bear. Bears today are regarded as a spiritual omen, usually unfavorable, held in fear and awe by the tribe.

The Bear Lodge of the Kiowas is known today as Devil's Tower National Monument. It is a mighty formation of columnar rock a thousand feet across the base, rising 865 feet upward to its mesa-like top, which is 275 feet across. Standing 5,117 feet above sea level, it served for centuries as a landmark to tribes in the Black Hills and beyond.

By 1700 the Kiowas had smoked the peace pipe and sealed a treaty with the Crows, who taught them much about the northern Plains culture and use of the buffalo-skin tipi. The Kiowas intermarried with the Crows; Chief Kicking Bird of later times was part Crow. A special sacred arrow (lance) in Tabguadal's family came from the Crows. More importantly, however, the Crows gave the Kiowas the sacred Tai-may for their Sun Dance.

The Kiowas held in reverence the power that Pahy, the sun, received from the Earth-maker and passed on to Tah'-lee, but they did not worship the sun. According to legend, about 1765 Pahy chose the Kiowas to be the final keepers of the Tai-may, the symbol of his power. The Tai-may was a partial female image nearly two feet long, and it was immediately incorporated into the sacred thanksgiving ceremony which the Kiowas called the *Daw-s'tome* (Procession-entering-the-lodge) or *Skaw-tow* (Cliff, or Protection, lodge) dance. The Crows and Dakotas gave it the popular name of Sun Dance. The Kiowas had no word meaning Sun Dance.[22]

Each summer about the time of the solstice the Kiowas held their Sun Dance. A family would send a chosen member into the sacred medicine lodge to dance in thanksgiving for the recovery of health, for example, or in gratitude for the safe return of a war party. Thanks for the Tai-may's protection was shown first in the form of a gift, possibly a blanket, and then by a dance in the lodge.

To preserve the sanctity of the Sun Dance lodge, which housed both the sacred Tai-may and the head of the sacrificial buffalo with an eagle perched atop, the warrior society called Elks guarded it. Later the Big Shields, another warrior society, assumed the guardian responsibility. After 1838 five Kiowa warrior societies took turns at providing protection during the Sun Dance.[23]

The "Buffalo Chase" performed during the dance re-created the ancient pre-horse method of hunting. A man on foot chased the herd downwind into the hidden tribal circle. While in the Yellowstone country, the Kiowas had hunted the buffalo, although the herds apparently deserted the region during the winter for lack of forage in the deep snow.

An elaborate set of rituals governed the entire ten days of the dance. Tribal elders recall that there were twenty-eight family groups repre-

Kots-a-to-ah by George Catlin (1832). Nearly seven feet tall, he was the swiftest of all Kiowa warriors, being able to run down buffaloes on foot and kill them with a knife or lance. The illustration shows the pre-horse culture shield, three feet in diameter, used by the Kiowas. The Khe-ate or Big Shields band of Kiowa foot soldiers preserved the name and tradition until after the last Sun Dance was held in 1887.

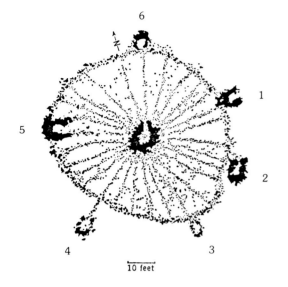

Wyoming Medicine Wheel. *The plan of the Medicine Wheel with cairn numbers added is from a 1958 survey.* Courtesy Science, 7 June 1974, Vol. 184, No. 4141; "Astronomical Alignment of the Big Horn Medicine Wheel" by John A. Eddy.

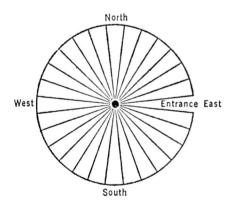

Sun Dance Medicine Lodge. From The Sacred Pipe, J. E. Brown, Ed. Copyright 1953 by the University of Oklahoma Press.

sented in the early Sun Dance. The camp circle faced east, and the medicine lodge was in the center. A position to the northwest of the medicine lodge called the "holy of holies" was used by priests to paint the bodies of the dancers. The Head Priest had a lodge position immediately to the southwest of the medicine lodge.

In the Big Horn Mountains of northern Wyoming is a well-worn travois trail leading to a huge stone Medicine Wheel laid out long ago on an exposed side of Medicine Mountain above the timberline. The local tribes today recall that the Medicine Wheel was there when they came, and their tradition relates it to the sun. Scientists using carbon dating on the artifacts estimate it came into existence sometime between 1700 and 1760, but incline to the later date.[24]

In 1962 Jacob Ahtone, a Kiowa working in the Bureau of Indian Affairs at Billings, Montana, suspected that the Medicine Wheel had been constructed by his tribe. He invited a tribal delegation, including Louis Toyebo, Stephen Poolant, and Richenda Toyebo, daughter of a priest of the old Kiowa Ghost Dance called Afraid-of-the-Bear, to inspect the site. In 1963 a combined delegation of Kiowas and Comanches revisited the Medicine Wheel. In addition to Ahtone and Toyebo, the Kiowas who checked the site were Price Spotted Horse, William Tanedoah, and Linn Pauahty and his wife Edna Hokeah. The Comanche delegates agreed that the area had been Kiowa territory long ago.

Fashioned in an area lacking timber for the annual Sun Dance medicine lodge, the Medicine Wheel appears as a two-dimensional replica of the wooden structure. The "wheel" is a stone pattern on the surface of the ground. In its center is a stone cairn, beneath which is a conical hole in the bedrock about a meter deep. Apparently the hole held the vertical lodge pole on which the buffalo head was traditionally placed.

From this central cairn are twenty-eight spokes radiating out to the rim of the wheel. Each radiating rock line or "supporting pole" represents one of the twenty-eight Kiowa family groups then existing. By 1867 only twenty-five groups remained in six Kiowa bands.

The "lodge" entrance opens to the east on the wheel's rim. Also placed at irregular intervals on the rim are six cairns which have mystified scholars for decades. If the wheel were Kiowa in origin, cairn one perhaps represents the ceremonial drum position that was always near the lodge entrance. Cairn two possibly is the guard location for the Kogui (Elks) or the Kiñep (Big Shields), traditional guardians for the Sun Dance until 1838.

Cairn three remains a puzzle; that it may have served as a spot for the assistant to the Head Priest is only speculation. Cairn four, the only cairn outside the wheel's rim, probably represents the separate location for the Head Priest since it coincides exactly with his traditional southwest location.

Cairn five on the northwest rim also coincides with the lodge known to the Kiowas as the "holy of holies," where the priests painted the bodies of the dancers. Cairn six also remains a mystery. Some tribal elders believe that the Kiowas built and used the Medicine Wheel, possibly during their migration to the Black Hills.[25] Others speculated it is Shoshone or Crow in origin.

Lending credence to the Kiowa claim are Kiowa place names in the region: *Kaui-kope* (Gai-k'op) or Kiowa Mountains in Montana; and the Wyoming townsite of Spotted Horse. Not far away in northeastern Wyoming is the great protruding rock monolith known in Kiowa legend as the Bear's Lodge. These locations are on the Kiowa migration route.

As the Kiowas moved across the northern Plains, they gradually discarded many cultural traits associated with their former life in the higher land of the Rockies. They adapted to the nomadic horse and buffalo culture with its mobility and exciting challenges. The new hunting life on the Plains produced a cultural revolution among the Kiowas, changing their way of life drastically. As the automobile permanently altered life for the white man two centuries later, the horse and buffalo caused the red man to introduce new behavioral patterns throughout every dimension of his culture.

The horse culture expanded the tribal range for hunting and war expeditions which produced greater economic wealth and military power. Before their great trek ceased, the Kiowas hunted and raided from the Rocky Mountains to central Arkansas, from the Dakotas to Mexico. The hunter on horseback easily chased down the buffalo, and only when the horse and rider closed in for the kill was there danger. The skilled Kiowa horsemen with their carefully trained horses developed the buffalo kill into an art.

The hunter's weapons also changed, the shields became smaller and bows shorter for use on horseback. Women developed new skills such as making rawhide covered saddles and rawhide harnesses, which they decorated with artistic designs. The Kiowas utilized every part of the buffalo: food from the flesh; cradles from skins over parallel boards; cord from sinews for bow strings and for binding both arrow points and feathers to the arrow shaft; awls from bones; jugs from bladders; buckets from paunches; spoons and powder flasks from horns; robes, shirts, dresses, moccasins, and tipi covers from skins; parfleches (rawhide envelopes) to carry dried strips of meat, berries, and cherries, flour for berry cakes from the underscraping of hides; burial winding sheets from skins for the dead; and braided ropes from the hair.

Horses became prized possessions, standards of value measuring the worth of other goods. To demonstrate their good intentions, warriors gave horses to the parents of girls they wanted to marry, and the parents reciprocated with similar gifts. Kiowa men spent more time on raids for horses, which often provoked retaliatory raids and warfare. Special rituals prepared the men for the raids and warfare; old ceremonial dances and rituals were adapted or new dances and songs were composed to celebrate the completion of successful ventures.[26]

Kiowa Parfleche of the nineteenth century. Kiowas kept clothes in this decorated parfleche. Undecorated parfleches were used to store beans, berries, and other food items. All parfleches contained a repellant to keep out insects.
Courtesy Smithsonian Institution.

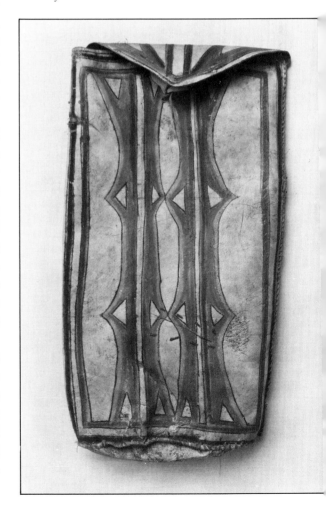

Learning to Hunt by Ha-goon (Silverhorn, 1892), showing wounded buffalo goring the horse of a hunter. Not an unusual occurrence if the hunter was not skilled. Courtesy Fort Sill Museum.

A warrior celebrated coups gained by being the first to strike a live enemy in combat, being the first to strike an enemy killed in combat by an arrow or other weapon, or being the second to strike a live enemy in combat. Great honors, but not coups, were gained by defying enemy fire at close range, rescuing a wounded comrade in battle, leading a successful war party, stealing a horse from an enemy camp, or riding on many war parties.[27] Kiowa tipi pictures, sometimes referred to as ''chronicle painting,'' record daring achievements of warriors.[28] Wartime exploits were also shown in Kiowa art.[29]

War parties observed certain rituals and rules of conduct. An act of bravery in war required witnesses who would testify before the tribe as to the truth of the coup. When a warrior returned from a revenge raid with an enemy scalp, he suspended the scalp from a pole or lance for all to see. He then described his exploit to the tribe and listened to the corroborative testimony from his associates. The women's *Awl-daw-ghoon-gah*, or Scalp Dance, in honor of his daring success, initiated the remainder of the celebration. But if a single warrior failed to return, the raid was considered a failure. Instead of the Scalp Dance, the lost warrior's father, grandfather, or his warrior society initiated the "Mourning Song" which was shared by the tribe.[30]

As the Kiowas became part of the horse and buffalo culture, they experienced the feeling of being larger than life. This sense of exhilaration was reflected in their Buffalo Dance. The songs and dances reveal the emotional response of a people to their new feeling of unlimited power.

The *P'-haw-goon*, or Buffalo Dance, originated when the Kiowas first discovered the many uses of the buffalo, possibly prior to 1680. The purpose of the dance was to appease the Buffalo Guardian Spirit. The buffalo symbolized power and the courage to fight to the death. Before a war or raiding party left camp, the Kiowas danced the Buffalo Dance and implored the Buffalo Guardian Spirit to give them the courage to fight to the death if necessary.[31]

The Kiowas eventually left the Black Hills and their Crow friends, moving first to the forks of the Platte and then even farther southward in 1775. Around 1790 a trader in New Mexico arranged for a Kiowa chief, Kooy-skaw-day (Wolf-lying-down), and the Comanche leader, Pareiya (Afraid-of-water), to discuss peace. The tribes made a friendship pact lasting to the present. The alliance between the larger Comanche tribe and the Kiowas and Kiowa-Apaches enabled the three to become the masters of the southern Plains. They lived, hunted, and raided together from 1790 until the 1867 Treaty of Medicine Lodge Creek, when all three were assigned to the same reservation.

With their Comanche allies, the Kiowas swept the southern Plains east of the Rocky Mountains from Kansas southward deep into Mexico. In the north they fought but eventually became friends with the Arapahos, Shoshonis, and the Arikara-Mandan-Hidatsa group; in the east and south, with the Wichita confederation of Wichitas, Tawakonis, Taovayas, and Wacos; in Texas, the Kichais. They made an uneasy truce with the Mescalero Apaches and a binding friendship with the Pueblos of New Mexico.

Enemies of the Kiowas on the Plains were the Comanches (until 1790), Cheyennes (until 1840), Pawnees, Dakotas (Sioux), and the Osages (until 1834). To the west they fought with the Utes, Navahos, and Jicarilla Apaches. In Texas they warred with the Caddos and Tonkawas.

As they fought and traveled through the prairie heartland of the North

The Old Warrior and Enemy Scalp by *James Auchiah (1929)*. *Courtesy a private collection.*

Kiowa Buffalo Hunt by Stephen Mopope
(1930). A skilled hunter always
approached from the buffalo's right side
for an arrow kill, and from the left for
a lance kill. The hunter aimed for the
unprotected space immediately behind
the shoulder and before the beginning of
the rib cage.
Courtesy Indian Arts and Crafts Board,
the U.S. Department of the Interior.

Kiowa Warriors Traveling the War Path by
White Buffalo.
Courtesy Towana Spivey.

American continent, the Kiowas enjoyed the murmuring water sanctuaries and the endless grasslands abounding with game. They contemplated imponderables — green and growing things in the spring and summer, racing deer, sturdy buffalo, the deep blue eternity of space, inspiring rainbows and sunsets, red sand and stone. During the fall and winter they listened to the cry of tiny birds, the honking of geese overhead, and they watched the crystalline ice form in canyon streams.

The Kiowa sensitivity to earthly beauty amidst the Plains culture found expression in their famous "Wind Songs." The *Gomda Dawgyah*, or wind song, was sung by the grandmother for the young man away on the warpath. As she thought of him far away, she considered the beautiful maiden waiting for him in camp as his prize.

WIND SONG
(Gomda Dawgyah)

The land is great.
When man travels on it
  he will never reach land's end;
But because there is a prize offered
To test a man to go as far as he dares,
He goes because he wants to discover his limits.[32]

The young brave and his companions discovered their limits on hunting parties or by counting "coup" in battle. Upon returning to camp, they received the adulation of their beautiful maidens and other tribal members. To support their coup counting and the Plains code of honor, the men developed warrior or soldier societies. The Polanyup, or Rabbits, enlisted boys from eight to twelve years old who desired to learn the ways of adult warriors. From twelve to approximately eighteen years of age they were in the Adaltoyup (Young Wild Sheep) society. Upon proving their manhood by counting coup, they entered one of the six adult Kiowa warrior societies.

Young Rabbit "Moving Camp" *by Roland Whitehorse.*

Each society had distinct dances and songs. Of the six societies, only the Tiah-pah with its Koitsenko, the Black Legs Society, and the struggling Ohoma Society have survived. Today young Rabbits and Sheep may graduate into these societies through family ties.

In the horse and buffalo days, the Rabbits had their *Polah-yee-gah*, or Rabbit Dance. Beginning in the early morning, the Rabbits emerged from their little tipis wearing tribal costumes and discharged certain camp duties under the direction of an adult leader. Then they performed their own dances and songs, as they still do.[33]

Both at camp festivals and in their homes, the Kiowas preserve many of their old songs. The *Gomda-dawgyah* tune entitled "That Wind" is a familiar Kiowa song, inciting nostalgic memories of the prairie tribal camp during winter. The wind whistled through the lodgepoles, blow-

ing the flaps, while the family played games and sang songs within the tipi. Today, as long ago, both the Wind Song and the succeeding lullaby song are sung by grandparents to their grandchildren.

THAT WIND, THAT WIND

That wind, that wind
Shakes my tipi, shakes my tipi
And sings a song for me,
And sings a song for me.[34]

This Kiowa lullaby, so old that its origin has been lost in antiquity, remains a perennial favorite:

THERE IS A BABY COMING
(Kiowa lullaby)

There's a baby coming
It's swimming in the water,
It's just like a little rabbit
She's got little rabbit feet.[35]

Kiowa Warrior's Dance by Stephen Mopope (1933). Note the roach headdress and eagle-feather fan of the dancer. Courtesy University of Oklahoma Museum of Art.

Lone Wolf's Winter Camp (1867). Photo by William S. Soule. Courtesy Smithsonian Institution.

The Tian-paye (Tiah-pah) society developed the Kiowas' famous *Goon-gah* dance, mislabelled the Gourd Dance by non-Kiowas and sometimes called the "Dog Soldiers' Dance" by other tribes. The dance utilized the "Red Wolf" legend, wherein a lone Kiowa raider was given the dance and songs by a red wolf. The dance accumulated an elaborate set of rituals from several membership groups which included the whip, rope, bugle, and gourd rattles — all possessing a legendary relationship to Kiowa acts of bravery. Kiowa war and raiding deeds were recreated in the symbols, dances, and songs. The dancers were men, the warriors and active protectors of the tribe.[36]

The *Ohoma* or Warrior's Dance was performed after successful war expeditions. Oral tradition says the dance was given to the Kiowas by the Cheyennes in the mid-nineteenth century. The Cheyennes had received it from the Omaha tribe, hence the Kiowa corruption of the name for the lodge preserving the dance. The Ohoma Dance was a northern Plains ceremony made up of many separate dances and songs: an Opening Song, a Charging Song; a Feast (Kettle) Song; a Tail Feather (Ritual) Song with its unusual flute dancers; a Mourning Song; a Give-away Song; and a Closing Song. Again the dances and songs recall symbolically the great deeds performed by many Kiowa warriors of long ago.[37]

The Koitsenko were the ten bravest Kiowa warriors. Their society was organized at the same time as the Tiah-pah, after a long battle with enemy tribes. Paw-Tawdle (Poor Buffalo) was an early Koitsenko leader, and he established their concepts for courage and honorable death. The minimum membership requirements were twenty-five war expeditions and ten coups gained by striking live enemies in hand-to-hand combat.

Another warrior fraternity, the Black Legs Society, recalls the traditional ceremonial practice of each warrior painting his legs black prior to the societal dance. Other distinguishing symbols of the society are the Sash and Sacred Arrow (actually a lance); the Red Cape; the Coup Stick; and the Roach Headdress. Each symbol recalls acts of incredible bravery by past Kiowa heroes and emphasizes the behavior expected of the societal members. The *T'ow-kow-ghat* or Black Legs Dance depicts the leader dismounting and pinning his sash to the ground with the Sacred Arrow. Anchored to the spot, he fought until he gained victory or death, or until another warrior released him. Songs from this dance are revered by the tribe. Seconds before he was shot to death, Sitting Bear (Sate'-awgha, or Satank) remarked that he would soon be smoking the pipe with his dead son "on the other side." Then he sang the revered Koitsenko death song:

> *Even though I live now,*
> *I will not live forever.*
> *Only the Sun and the Earth*
> *remain forever.*[38]

Black Legs Dancers. *Dixon Palmer (right) and unidentified dancer at Anadarko, Oklahoma, 1968. Courtesy Jane Pattie.*

During the height of Kiowa power, their dances became artistic expressions of the Kiowa concept of the entire life process translated into human experience. The traditional Kiowa temperament is still reflected through dance rituals. Tribal memory expressed through symbols powerfully influences dance.

Kiowa dances are, therefore, suggestive and symbolic. Not always presenting the complete symbol, the dance may hint of a greater subject. The dance contains a power that is mystical, even magical. Excellent dance, like excellent painting, is an example of "good spirit" and helps the individual Kiowa to achieve a feeling of oneness with the universal spirit force.

As the Kiowas danced and roamed free amidst nature's bounty, discordant notes arose as the tribe faced the white man's expansion onto the fenceless plains. Responding to these new pressures, Kiowa story tellers related Saynday legends around the lodge fires during the long winter nights. The legends told how Saynday protected his people from the ravages of enemy raiders and the white man's smallpox. In a series of humorous domestic tales, Saynday taught men to beware of "whirlwind women" and to court potentially good wives. The values in these ever popular tales did not reflect a morality beyond reach.

Saynday lingered on earth only long enough to show his people how to trick the white man, but not how to defeat him. When Saynday finally left this earth, he soared outward on the wind. Today, it is said, the five fingers on his right hand may be seen as stars in the Orion constellation.

Buffalo Dancer *by Blackbear Bosin (1947).*
Kiowa painting, like Kiowa music, is
symbolic and suggestive of larger topics
and more universal feelings than can be
captured on a single canvas.
Courtesy Philbrook Art Center.

4 Rainy Mountain and Great Medicine

His spirit finds its way
into the spirit world,
Lifted on the wind above the grandeur
and beauty of the earth.

> — *Yellow Wolf*[39]

THE KIOWA MIGRATION ENDED AT Rainy Mountain. In the land of the Washita River in Oklahoma the people stretched out on the prairie floor, closed their eyes and dreamed, their cares forgotten. They drank in the scene of the earth, heard the sound of the wind, felt the warmth of the sun, and listened to the exuberant song of joy within their souls. They hoped never to leave this place of peace.

Even today the scene is little changed from a century ago. At the last light of day, nature makes speedy leaps of beauty. Filmy clouds rapidly change from silver to apricot to rose-grape. The lone mountain, like a sentinel, becomes light brown, then purple, and finally mauve. The Earth-maker continually gives his people a sign, even as he did at Bear Lodge. The Kiowas observe these changing wonders of nature, knowing that tomorrow another wondrous event called dawn will reveal new scenes of magnificence. The unfolding beauty of nature—the parade of life—provides sustenance for the individual spirit; the sensation of the presence of the spirit force is overwhelming.

At historic Medicine Rock in south-central Oklahoma, a towering ledge protrudes against the sky. Though vast in its expanse, the site exudes serenity. It is a magic place where, long ago, the medicine man waved his hand over this bend of the Washita River and forbade noises to intrude upon his meditation. It was a place apart, a world rediscovered. Medicine Bend offered peace and reflection to the owl man. His evenings were memorable, each an affirmation of renewal. Here the vision might come to him. In this natural sanctuary the medicine man captured a single moment of eternal truth, blending atmosphere and environment with the delicate threads of dreams discovered and wishes fulfilled.

The white man has never understood this private miracle of the Kiowa mind. In his mental sanctuary the medicine man entered another plane of existence, where he experienced the oneness of past, present, and future. Here in this humbling yet inspiring environment his mind and spirit became one with the universal mind and spirit. The visionary moment of inspiration enabled him to continue on his way, refreshed and certain of his purpose.

The Kiowa medicine man possessed special powers. His medicine bundle contained personal items and those handed down from his ancestral predecessors, and each item contained spirit power. He was a prophet and healer, a maker of magic power and, in rare instances, of curses. He dealt with sacred things.[40]

THE KIOWA RANGE, 1820-1874

Adapted from Mayhall, The Kiowas, p. 193.

Ta-ne-haddle (Running Bird), *once a keeper of one of the Buffalo Medicine bundles, was one of the last Kiowa Buffalo Medicine Cult members. As a young man his name was Pauahty (Walking Buffalo) but later he gave his name to his nephew, Dominic Tahbone, and took his second name, Running Bird. Courtesy KHRS.*

Sacredness is abstract; its manifestation comes in many forms and styles. The majesty of the Kiowa buffalo medicine man (mistakenly called buffalo priest by some) was understood even if his symbolic acts and the objects in his medicine bag were strange to the individual beholder. The objects may have been as disparate as a rooster's head, a snake skin, a buffalo tail, dried sage, and a colored rock. But each item contained a special force, or power, known only to the holder of the medicine bundle. From the items he drew strength. The imagery contained in his symbolic gestures spoke to the universal sense of miracle held by all Kiowas, but only the buffalo medicine men had the power or the right to perform the Buffalo Medicine Cult Dance. From 1822 until early in the twentieth century, it was their prerogative to do so. When the last Kiowa medicine man died, the performing dance died with him.[41]

The *P'-haw-eey-ghun,* or Buffalo Medicine Cult Dance, dates back to 1822. In that year, according to tradition, a Kiowa woman escaped from her Pawnee captors. By traveling at night and hiding by day she eluded her pursuers. One day during a terrible storm she sought refuge inside a buffalo carcass lying on the plains and she received the buffalo power. The Buffalo Woman brought the needed buffalo power, or medicine, to the Kiowas; later she gave the buffalo power to the Kiowa medicine men in separate bundles.[42]

5 The End of the Buffalo Culture

The day of gaining honor in war had disappeared;
  I could not teach my children the old ways
  of war and honor.
The government agent instructed me to return home
  and tell my people that the Road of Honor was one
  of hard work by good, obedient men and women.
                    — *Ta-ne-haddle (Running Bird)*[43]

IN AN INCREDIBLY SHORT TIME THE Kiowas lost the world they knew, the hunting and wandering life centered around the horse and the buffalo. After the Treaty of Medicine Lodge Creek in 1867 some Kiowa bands and the Quahadi Comanches refused to accept slow death by starvation on the reservation. By the fall of 1874 the southern Plains were crossed and recrossed by many columns of United States troops who allowed the Kiowas and Comanches no time to hunt or to rest their ponies.

While some Kiowas gave up the hopeless struggle and returned to the agency, others sought refuge on the Staked Plains of Texas. They hid in one of their favorite camping grounds at Elk Creek in Palo Duro Canyon. There Colonel Ranald S. Mackenzie's scouts discovered them. After an all night march the troops descended the canyon trails at daybreak. The warriors held off the soldiers while the women and children escaped, but the troops captured and killed most of the horses and mules before the Indians could recapture them. On foot, without lodges or food, some without robes or weapons, the Kiowas and Comanches were drenched by torrential rains. In small parties they straggled back to the agency and surrendered. The Kiowas were horseless; their glory days had ended as winter descended.

Now confined to a reservation, the Kiowas faced a bleak future. The huge herds of buffalo soon vanished before the onslaught of white hunters, who killed them only for sport or for their hides, leaving the flesh to rot. It was beyond the Kiowas' comprehension that the buffalo would be killed in so wasteful a manner; it was beyond the Kiowa vision of man's relation to earth and nature's creatures.

By the summer of 1879 the Kiowas could not find a single buffalo on the southern Plains for their Sun Dance. A Kiowa calendar pictograph for that summer shows a horse's head above the Sun Dance medicine lodge instead of the ceremonial buffalo's head. The Kiowas ate their horses that year to keep from starving.

The Kiowas became increasingly dependent upon government rations dispensed by their agent or from Fort Sill. In 1887 they held their last Sun Dance. In 1890 a gathering for the dance was dispersed by troops even before the ceremonies started. Without the horse and buffalo, without their song and dance, the Kiowas lost their cultural identity.

Horse-eating Sun Dance (*Dohasan calendar, summer 1879*). *The bison were so scarce that the Kiowas killed their ponies for food. After this year the location and killing of a single bison was a rare event in Kiowa territory.*

Kiowa Submission to the Agency by Robert Redbird. After their horses had been killed by troopers, the hungry and destitute Kiowas returned to the agency during the fall and winter of 1874. Courtesy James and Helen McCorpin.

A tribe overrun and engulfed by more numerous adversaries with superior weapons understandably suffered deep psychological wounds. Despair and hopelessness formed a shroud over the Kiowas as their hunting grounds were denied them, their religious ceremonies outlawed, and their social system uprooted. Desperate, they were ready to grasp at any straw of hope. For the Kiowas, a revivalist and messianic movement arose in the 1880s in the form of *Awh-mai-goon-gah*, the Feather Dance, but called the Ghost Dance by many other tribes and by white men.[44]

The revival began with the visions and preaching of Wovoka, a Paiute in Nevada. The time was coming, he said, when the Indians, living and dead, would be together again and live as they had before the coming of the whites. The buffalo too would return. Wovoka's message brought hope to an oppressed and hungry people.

"You must not fight," Wovoka ordered. "Do no harm to anyone. Do right always. When your friends die, you must not cry."[45] In order to fulfill his prophecy, he called for all Indians regularly to perform the Ghost Dance and its songs. Then one day the earth would tremble and all the whites would be swept away. Those who participated in the Ghost Dance moved in a circle, singing the songs Wovoka had prescribed. Some fell in a trance and later arose to tell wonderful tales of visits with dead relatives.

The dance spread from the home of the Paiute in Nevada to the Plains tribes. Even though Wovoka had said that they must not fight, the Sioux on the Northern Plains and the Arapahos on the Southern Plains danced in symbolically painted Ghost Dance shirts allegedly impenetrable by the white man's bullets. An Arapaho prophet named Sitting Bull — not to be confused with the Sioux chief of the same name — brought the dance and message to the Kiowas. Some Kiowas adapted the dance as their Feather Dance, but Chief Ahpea-taw or Apiatan (Wooden Lance) and others opposed it.

Hoping to see his beloved son who had recently died, Apiatan had traveled to Nevada to visit Wovoka. Disappointed in this hope and convinced that Wovoka was not the prophet many tribes thought him to be, Apiatan advised the Kiowas to forget the Ghost Dance. Many followed his advice, but others continued dancing.[46]

The white people became alarmed at the dance, especially the songs, an example being *I Shall Cut Off His Feet*:

> *I shall cut off his feet,*
> *I shall cut off his head,*
> *He shall arise again.*[47]

The song referred to the dismembered buffalo and its promised resurrection. Misunderstanding its meaning, whites asked for and received troops to disrupt dance ceremonies throughout the Plains.

Apiatan (Wooden Lance, 1890).
Courtesy Smithsonian Institution.

Buffalo Hunt *by Al Momaday (1958). The single warrior chosen to kill the buffalo for the Kiowa Sun Dance took only two arrows, but he planned to use only one for a clean kill and thereby reduce the loss of blood. A sloppy, bloody kill was a bad omen.*
Courtesy Indian Arts and Crafts Center, the U.S. Department of the Interior.

The Sioux suffered most from the military response to the Ghost Dance. One band of Sioux resisted the intrusion and fled to the Badlands. Another band saw its leader, Sitting Bull, killed by Indian police from Standing Rock agency. Big Foot's band, en route out of the Badlands, was intercepted by troops of the Seventh Cavalry. The Indians surrendered and camped at Wounded Knee. The next day the troops were ordered to disarm the Sioux. A medicine man, Yellow Bird, blew on his eagle-bone whistle and urged the Sioux to resist. A fight began, and at least one hundred men and twice as many women and children were killed or fatally wounded. The Ghost Dance shirts had failed to protect them from the bullets.

The Kiowas fared somewhat better with the Federal Government than the Sioux bands, for they never accepted the Ghost Dance in the Arapaho-Sioux form and content. They carefully distinguished their dance as the "Feather Dance" because of its non-militant character and by the single upright feather worn on the back of the participant's head. The dance was held in January and July almost every year from 1890 to 1916. During the ceremony the Kiowas prayed to Dom-oye-alm-daw-k'hee, the Earth-maker.

Even though the Feather Dance was completely peaceful, the Federal Government opposed it and finally withheld the tribal rations until the Kiowas agreed to discontinue it. The dream of a return to the glory days of warriors and buffaloes faded and died.[48]

6 The Search for Identity

Finally there was no place of refuge,
*   no personal retreat for peace of mind.*
I was on the edge of the world,
*   but the pressures were still there.*
Only personal imagination and visions,
*   memories of the past,*
*   remained to free my spirits.*
Only this memory kept my dignity alive.

—Monroe Tsatoke[49]

WITH THE DEMISE OF THE FEATHER DANCE, some Kiowas preserved their spiritual hopes in peyotism. Since peyotism is the strongest religious cult today among all Native Americans, it carries the appropriate name of the Native American Church. Peyotism represents the red man's attempt to resolve the dilemma of coexisting in the white man's world while remaining spiritually independent. Through peyote worship the Kiowa participant attempts to preserve both culture and sanity in the one-sided cultural struggle.

The ceremony begins at sunset in a white tipi with the Peyote Priest and the participants seated around a crescent-shaped altar representing the moon. In the center of the altar a large peyote button rests on a bed of sage. The Peyote Road is symbolized by a line drawn the length of the crescent. A flickering fire ritually laid before the altar lights the lodge.

In contemplation and prayer the communicant partakes of the peyote. Each individual seeks a personal communion with the Spirit Power, and peyote is the sacrament. The participant prays to *Sayn-daw-kee*, or Peyote Powerful Spirit. The visual world and the spirit world mentally become one again as beautifully colored visions induced by the hallucinogenic peyote reaffirm unity. As the participant smokes the communal pipe and sings the peyote songs, the feeling of wholeness returns. His spirit floats on the wind. Visions of past tribal glory arise in the spiraling smoke. Within the white lodge the Kiowa knows the meaning of his identity. His hopes soar, as does the symbolic cormorant bird associated with peyotism. The place where dreams are born is found within the heart.[50]

And so the folk memory persists. Today the Kiowas gather and dance, celebrating their collective lives, expressing their spirit as a tribe. They have always done so. This memory keeps their dignity alive.

Cormorant Bird. The symbolic messenger bird carrying prayers of the Peyote participants to the Great Powers.
Courtesy Ta-ne-shyahn (Little Bird).

7 Cultural Preservation

We, the old chiefs,
  are looking down;
We leave you these songs
  and this dance
For you to preserve.
      —Old Kiowa Song[51]

ORAL LANGUAGE SUSTAINED THE KIOWAS for generations, preserving their culture and their identity. Should knowledge of the language die, many wonderful traditions preserved in the expressive power of the language would die also. Hundreds of years of tribal meaning and beliefs, wrapped in the untranslatable emotional content of Kiowa words, would be lost forever.

Between 1500 and 1980, half of the North American Indian languages disappeared. Today others are rapidly declining, especially since the mass media of radio, television, and movies are bombarding Indian societies through daily contact. Nearly all contact is in the English language. Concerned over the demise of their native tongue, Kiowa tribal elders hope at least to preserve much of their cultural heritage in English translation. Whether the heritage ever appears in the Kiowa language is for the current generation of young Kiowas to decide.

The Kiowa language has one dialect without any variations. There are six vowels with nasal counterparts. There are three diphthongs and twenty-three consonants, but no letter r. Kiowa verbs have only the past, present, and future tenses in both the positive and negative. The first person singular pronoun also serves as the plural, and the third person does not exist. The numerical count is decimal.

The Kiowa language has never been fully recorded. No dictionary exists, nor has the spelling of Kiowa words ever been standardized, or even agreed upon by the tribe. Each Kiowa discussant pronounces and then spells phonetically. Wide spelling variations inevitably result.

Spelling complications arise because the spoken language contains sucking and clicking sounds, two loudnesses and a pitch accent with different syllables of a word receiving high, low, or falling pitches. There are also non-rhythmic popping and nasal sounds which almost defy translation into written form. In recent years under the leadership of Charley and Carrie Redbird, William Wolfe, Louis Toyebo, Linn Pauahty and others, some Kiowas have attempted to use the phonetic "Grinnell system" to simplify the spelling of Kiowa words. In many instances this system of spelling words as they sound has been used in this study. A brief explanation follows which demonstrates how part of the system applies to the reading of Kiowa words.

Vowel Symbols	As in English	As in Kiowa	
aw	saw	haw	"yes"
ow	low	tow	"house"
oo	boot	koot	"book"
ee	see	kee	"meat"
ay	day	towday	"shoe"
ah	ah	ahdaw	"tree"

When the vowel ah follows y, it is pronounced like the vowel a in the English word "cat"; examples are the Kiowa words gyah-paw (it is cheap) and shyahn (little).

Four of the six vowels listed may be followed by the letter y, so that syllables may end in awy, owy, ooy, and ahy; Kiowa examples are kawy-towgyah (Kiowa words), tsowy (coffee), kooy (wolf), and pahy (sun).

An underlined vowel is spoken through the nose, as in the Kiowa word hawnay (no). Also any vowel which occurs next to a nasal consonant and in the same syllable is spoken through the nose, even though it is not underlined; examples are the Kiowa words hawn (not), náw (I, we), and the last vowel of hawnay (no).

The letters b, d, and g are pronounced lightly.

The letters p, t, and k are pronounced without air, as in paghaw (one), tahday (eye), and kowt (strong).

The three diphthongs ph, th, and kh are pronounced with air, as in pheedaw (fire), thowday (leg), and khaw (blankets).

The accented letters p,' t,' and k' are pronounced with a popping sound, as in p'aw (moon), t'aw (spoon), k'ee (firewood), k'yahhee (man). An apostrophe (') is pronounced by holding one's breath between two parts of a word, as in how'awn (road), tsow'ah (he believes), and yah-thah'aw-may (he helped me).

The letter l is pronounced like the dl in the English word "cradle" or like the tl in "cattle" or al in gyan-sal (it is hot).

Tone is important in Kiowa, but in this volume only a few of the high-pitched syllables are marked with the high tone (´) over the vowel as in náw (I, we).[52]

Today as the Kiowa elders peel back the layers of the tribal mind, they expose the sensitive core of their cultural being through their traditional dances, songs, and legends. Emotion-filled memories of past challenge and achievement, moments of triumph and glory, are filed away in the ritual to sooth their troubled hearts.

An outsider listens while the great drum — the Voice of Thunder — sends out its compelling call. The stranger stands transfixed, unwilling to intrude in the song and dance, yet drawn toward the dancers and drum. Gradually he relaxes and discovers that the tribe not only forgives the intrusion but welcomes it. The people ask all to share their reality, their being. The dances, songs, and legends are part of that reality, rendered by the Kiowa elders.

Drummer-Singers by Jack Hokeah (1932), depicting use of a hand drum. The dress, not true Kiowa, reflects the Pueblo influence in New Mexico where Hokeah studied and painted for several years. Courtesy Oklahoma State Historical Society.

‖ THE CREATOR AND THE TAI-MAY

With a burst of heat Pahy appeared,
Brought to us by Saynday from the east.
Our people saw the glory of the Earth-maker's creation,
The visual earth spoke softly in nature's poetry,
And the Kiowas understood the power of the
  spirit force.

—*James Auchiah*[1]

I N THE BEGINNING DOM-OYE-ALM-DAW-K'HEE created the earth and all living things — mountains and prairies, streams and lakes, animals and Kiowas, night and day, sun and moon. The Earth-maker, the great omnipotent spirit of the universe, is a mystery. The Earth-maker is power. Some of this power is transmitted through Pahy, the sun.

Pahy chose the Kiowas as the final keepers of his power symbol, the sacred Tai-may. Highest in rank of all Kiowa spiritual medicines are the ten sacred medicine bundles and the Tai-may. The Kiowas acquired the Tai-may about 1765 by the white man's calendar.[2]

The Tai-may, an image of a female human figure without legs, is about two feet in length. Described differently by each generation of viewers, the Tai-may presumably is dressed in buckskin and adorned with fluffy white feathers; the figure wears on its head a large erect eagle plume feather with long ermine pendants attached at the base of the feather. Around the Tai-may's neck are several strands of blue beads. During the Sun Dance the Kiowa dancers in their spiritual quest viewed in reverential awe this sacred image of the sun's power.

The Kiowas acquired the Tai-may from an Arapaho who had received the figure from the Crows. According to the traditional legend, the event took place during a Sun Dance.

...i-may, The Kiowa sun power symbol for ...e Skaw-tow or Sun Dance. The Kiowas ...ll have the sacred Tai-may, an exact ...py of which was made by Pau-kei, the ...ndson of Red Otter, and presented to ...igh Lenox Scott who forwarded it to ...mes Mooney at the Smithsonian Institu-...n about seventy years ago. Pau-kei's ...other was a descendant of the original ...owa woman who married the old ...rapaho Tai-may keeper. ...urtesy Smithsonian Institution.

Tai-may Comes to the Kiowa

L ONG AGO IN THE NORTH THE CROWS held a Sun Dance. People from other tribes came to the Crow camp. A poor Arapaho with no horses or belongings attended the Sun Dance with his tribe. The Crow priest noticed how earnestly and long the poor old Arapaho danced before the Tai-may, praying for its help. Moved by pity for the Arapaho, the priest gave him the Tai-may image. The Crows, however, were angered because this great favor had been bestowed upon someone from another tribe. They acted threateningly toward the Arapaho, yet feared the great powers of their Sun Dance priest and permitted the Arapaho to depart with their Tai-may.

The old Arapaho now had new powers. People came to him from near and far. He accumulated wealth; his herd of ponies was larger than that of any other Arapaho or Crow. When the Crows held their next annual Sun Dance, he attended with his great drove of fine ponies, and the Crows were furious. Some jealous Crows decided to recover their Tai-may. They followed the old man on his return home after the dance. While the Arapaho slept on the first night of his journey, they stealthily approached his camp, removed the medicine bag containing the Tai-may from the pole in front of his tipi, and returned it to their tribe.

Discovering his loss the next morning, the Arapaho decided to stay in Crow territory rather than return home in disgrace. Eventually he made a duplicate of the Tai-may which he took back to his own tribe.* He later married a Kiowa woman and chose to live with her people. Thus he brought the Tai-may to the Kiowas.

Our people watched the Tai-may, saw it had great power, adopted it as our most sacred medicine, and regarded it as the most important symbol used in our great Skaw-tow (Sun Dance) ceremony. Although the Tai-may is ours, its Tho-adalta or keeper has always been a descendant of the Arapaho man and the Kiowa woman. For generations the keepers, by tribal tradition, have had some Arapaho blood.[3]

A-mai-ah, *the Kiowa Tai-may keeper from 1894 to 1939.*
Courtesy U.S. Army Field Artillery and Fort Sill Museum, Fort Sill, Oklahoma.

*Some claim he recovered the original.

They Cut Off Their Heads *(Dohasan calendar, summer 1833). The Osages, raiding a Kiowa camp while the warriors were gone, killed and beheaded a large number of Kiowa women, children, and elderly men. Since the Osages also stole the sacred Tai-may, no Sun Dance was held that summer. The picture shows a knife and head.*

Sun-power Medicine

When the Utes Killed Us *(Dohasan calendar, summer 1868). On a revenge party against the Navahos, the Kiowas were carrying two of their three sacred figures when a Ute war party defeated them and took the two small sacred figures, "man" and "woman", which were never returned. The pictograph shows the figure of a man holding out the stone war pipe which was sent around as an invitation to warriors to join an expedition.*

THE TAI-MAY IS STILL IN THE TRIBE, kept by A-mai-ah (E-mah-ah) from 1894 until her death in 1939, and currently held by her eldest granddaughter, Nina Kodaseet, who lives near Anadarko, Oklahoma.

Other power medicine has been associated with the Tai-may. One was a medicine bottle taken during a battle when the allied Kiowa-Comanche warriors attacked a Blackfoot camp and killed an enemy warrior; a Comanche captured his medicine.

Upon returning to his camp, the Comanche warrior hung the medicine bottle in his tipi. That night while the Comanche tried to sleep, the medicine bottle made strange noises. At sunrise the fearful Comanche gave it to a Kiowa friend. The Kiowa trimmed the bear kidney in the medicine bottle into the image of a small man, and the sounds ceased. Upon learning later that the Blackfoot medicine bottle had originally been part of the Tai-may medicine, the Kiowa gave the medicine to the Tai-may keeper, who reunited it with the Tai-may and the other image, an even smaller female figure called "woman." The Kiowas revered and tried to protect these sacred symbols, including the two smaller ones known only as "woman" and "man."[4] The story of the loss of the Tai-may is explained in the following legend.

ACCORDING TO OUR COUNT, WE LOST the Tai-may medicine the year of the Osage Cut-Throat Massacre (1833). The Kiowa warriors were away on a raiding party. Our women and children, guarded by a few old men, were camped in a secluded spot on Otter Creek at the base of Head Mountain, not far from Rainy Mountain in the Washita Mountains of Oklahoma. The Osage warriors crept up to the camp and killed nearly all of the inhabitants. During the slaughter the wife of the Tai-may priest attempted to untie the Tai-may medicine bag from the pole in front of the tipi and escape, but she was killed and the bag was captured by the Osages. We call this the "Cut-Throat Massacre" because the Osages cut off the heads of our people and placed them in our cooking kettles. For two years the Osages had our medicine. When peace was made between the two tribes in 1835, the Tai-may bag was returned to the Kiowa tribe.

To protect the Tai-may image in the future, our people decided never to take it into battle for fear it might again be captured. The two small images called "woman" and "man" were still carried into battle, and in 1868 the Utes captured them when Heap-of-Bears was killed while carrying them. These two smaller images were never recovered.

The Tai-may image has always been the mediator between our people and the Sun power. One of our prayers to the Tai-may shows that we know the Sun looks after his people.

> *The Creator above made you for life,*
> *We do not know him,*
> *We cannot see him wherever he is.*
> *But you know him,*
> *Ask him to give you power for our life.*[5]

THE TAI-MAY IMAGE AND ITS PRIESTLY KEEPER were identically painted during the annual Sun Dance when they both were in the medicine lodge. Their faces were painted with red and black zig-zag lines running downward from their eyes to indicate power from the sun. The keeper's body was painted the same shade of yellow as his deerskin shirt. The custom of using yellow probably originated from a dream by a keeper long ago, and its meaning is not known, although its color resembles the sun. The keeper, however, had a blue or green sun painted in the center of his chest and back, flanked on either side by two crescent moons. On his head was a jackrabbit skin cap with a breath-feather attached. During the Sun Dance the keeper held in his mouth an eagle-bone whistle from which dangled a large eagle feather. He clutched some live cedar in one hand, and sage was tied to both wrists. The *Prayer to the Sun*, given by the Tai-may keeper, suggests the symbolic importance of the cedar.

> *PRAYER TO THE SUN*
>
> *O Creator, you give us this tree,*
> *Cedar, because you love it.*
> *Every other tree dies, as does grass;*
> *But not this tree*
> *It does not die in winter,*
> *Its leaves do not drop in fall,*
> *We think you love it,*
> *You take care of it,*

You keep it always green,
You give it a good road,
I want you to smell its smoke.[6]

Like cedar, sage remains green all winter. The sacredness of both derives from their contrast to other vegetation, for the Creator has especially favored them with continuing life the year around. The smoke offering referred to in the last line of the prayer may best be explained later during the analysis of the annual Skaw-tow, or Kiowa Sun Dance.

‖ SKAW-TOW

The Sun Dance

The Cedar-Bluff Sun Dance, Summer 1859 (Dohasan Calendar). *The Kiowas kept pictographic calendars. The oldest surviving Kiowa calendar is that of Chief Dohasan I.*

When the horses grew fat from white sage grass,
It was the time for the Dance of Thanksgiving,
The Daw-s'tome, the Going-into-the-medicine-lodge dance,
For Pahy, our men, our families, our tribe.

—*Kickingbird*[1]

THE SPECTACULAR AND SACRED CEREMONY popularly called the Sun Dance was typical of most of the Plains tribes. The original Kiowa dance in the northern mountains and plains was a solemn and majestic ceremony which the tribe called a "dance of thirst and self-denial." It was related to the sun only at the moment of sunrise and sunset, when certain songs in the ceremonial ritual coincided with the action of the sun. Although the ritual was not concerned primarily with the sun, the dancers did stare incessantly at the sun or the medicine bundle at the top of the center lodgepole. The Dakotas called it the "sun-gazing" dance, which is probably how the name "Sun Dance" originated. The Kiowas call it the *Skaw-tow* (Cliff, or Protection, bank) or *Daw-s'tome* (Procession-entering-the-lodge) Dance. In the late nineteenth century, white men failed to hear the muted "S" and called it Ka-do instead of Skaw-tow.[2]

In the popular mind the Sun Dance is often associated with self-inflicted torture. Among most of the Plains tribes the young dancers had slits cut in the skin of their breasts or backs, and skewers were inserted under the cut flesh. If the skewers were in the dancers' breasts, they were tied by rawhide thongs to the central lodgepole. If the skewers were in their backs, they were attached to several buffalo skulls which the dancers dragged around the camp. The purpose was to tear through the flesh and gain release from the skewers without the dancers showing any pain. The dancers thereby demonstrated their courage and bravery.

The Kiowas did not include self-torture in their medicine dance. The cutting of flesh or shedding of blood during the Sun Dance was a tribal taboo. If by accident any blood was shed, the dancing would likely be concluded at that moment. Even the buffalo bull killed for the dance was mandatorily shot through the heart rather than the lungs, so that the animal would not bleed at the nose or mouth; excessive bleeding by the buffalo brought great sickness to the Kiowas.[3]

On the floor of the Sun Dance medicine lodge, the Kiowas drew the outline of a human body in the sand and poured the ashes from the Straight Pipe on the location of the heart. If this symbolic act was a carry-over from earlier days when the dance included self-torture, there is no record of it. Some writers have claimed that the dancers, who had the sun and moon painted on their chests and backs, cut permanent outlines of the designs on their bodies. Tribal elders, however, deny this allegation. If someone did mutilate his body, he did so independently of the Sun Dance because the shedding of blood, intentionally or accidentally, at the Kiowa Sun Dance was considered an evil omen.

Around the middle of the nineteenth century, an incident occurred at a Kiowa Sun Dance that might have been misinterpreted by outsiders. An account by the participant himself, the son of Chief Kickingbird, has recently been discovered.

T'ane-angópte (Kickingbird). A great Kiowa chief and Sun Dance participant, Kickingbird passed down his name and much of the Kiowa folk memory to Kickingbird II before his death in 1875. Photo by William S. Soule, 1868.
Courtesy Bureau of Indian Affairs and the National Archives.

Lost and Regained

A LONG TIME AGO, WHEN I WAS seven years old, my papa who loved me had a dream that I was inside a Sun Dance lodge. He saw me on the center pole; so when they held the Sun Dance that year, my father tied me on the center pole like Jesus crucified. I stayed there all day without food or drink. The center pole had a buffalo head tied on top, and the image of God (Tai-may) on one side. The image was made out of buckskin, face like mine, painted, eagle feathers hanging from the shoulders. The Indians danced around, about 300 outside the ring and about 50 inside. I cried and cried, but my papa said that I was

Poingya, son of Satank and a Kiowa med-
icine man, was the Tai-may priest in the
final years of the Kiowa Sun Dance. He
was the brother of Joshua Givens and
Julia Givens, the first wife of George Hunt.
Photo 1930.
Courtesy U.S. Army Field Artillery and
Fort Sill Museum.

Kiowa Sun Dance, Summer 1867 (Keah-ko
calendar). A Navaho who stole Kiowa
horses was hung from the Medicine Lodge
pole.

all right, that I would grow up a strong man like a fighting chief. At sundown my father cut me loose and gave
a feast. They all called me big chief, like a fighting
warrior.[4]

THE TAI-MAY KEEPER, WHO ANNOUNCED the ceremonies, held a
position of paramount importance at the Kiowa Sun Dance. During winter upon request of one or more tribal members inspired by a dream
vision, the Tai-may keeper decided whether to hold a Sun Dance the
following summer. When he decided favorably, he sent riders from his
camp to inform his people in the other camps when and where the
forthcoming Sun Dance would be held. All tribal members were
required to be present.

The announcement of the next Sun Dance was met with joy. This was
a dance of thanksgiving, as well as of supplication to the sun. For those
who had been spared in battle, had survived a serious illness, or had
been rewarded with good hunting, the dance was an expression of gratitude. For those whose family members needed to be healed, whose
women desired the blessing of children, whose camps needed food, or
whose tipis sought revenge from past transgressions and maltreatment
from their enemies—Utes, Pawnees, Dakotas, Cheyennes, Osages, Sauk
and Fox, Tonkawas, or Navahos—the Sun Dance ritual, with its dancing and singing, its drum beats and aroused emotions, offered strength
for the fulfillment of sacred vows for the new year.

Wherever the messengers of the Tai-may keeper traveled, they were
cheered when they approached the camps and gave the sign of the Sun
Dance. By imitating the blowing of the eagle whistle, looking upward at
the sun, and giving an up-and-down dance movement with the right
hand and shoulders in tune to the music of an imaginary drum and
whistle, the messengers made known their good news. Only the time
and place was added to this sign understood by all Native Americans
who participated in the Sun Dance. Those who received the sign knew
that the required presence of all tribal members strengthened tribal
bonds, served as a social gathering, provided courtship opportunities
for the young, and permitted vows to the sun to be strengthened and
hopefully fulfilled in the gathering of the different bands.

The Sun Dance was held about the time of the summer solstice, if
conditions permitted. Whenever the cottonwood trees began shedding
their white cotton fluff that floated their seeds, the Kiowas knew the
time was near. Or when the white sage grass was about a foot high and
the horses were fat, they knew the time had arrived. All of these conditions occurred in late June or early July.

The Tai-may keeper ordered the Sun Dance held in a convenient
location where everyone could reach the campsite within four days, in

accordance with the Kiowa sacred number four. Since ten additional days were required from the start of the ritual until the completion of ceremonies for camp abandonment, the site chosen for the dance was always near a sizable body of water with trees for shade and grass for horses.

The Kiowa Sun Dance usually included about ten days of tribal activity, including four to six "getting ready days" and four dancing days. Sun Dances held today by the Crows, Sioux, Northern Cheyennes, Bannock-Shoshones, and Utes last only two or two and a half days. The original dance has been greatly modified because public health regulations do not permit fasting for more than two days. The Kiowas have not held a Sun Dance since 1887, for the buffalo had disappeared and the Federal Government forbade the ceremony.

On the evening before the first of the six "getting ready" days presented herein, the Tai-may keeper would be informed that all had arrived for the ceremonies. He requested that a gentle and well trained horse be brought to him before sunrise the next morning. Then everyone in camp retired, anticipating the events of the next day.[5]

Kiowa Sun Dance, Summer 1873 (Keah-ko calendar). During this Sun Dance, Black Buffalo stole the wife of Appearing Wolf, who in turn shot some of Black Buffalo's horses.

THE FIRST "GETTING READY" DAY

At precisely sunrise of the next or first "getting ready" day, the Tai-may keeper dramatically appeared on horseback with the sacred Tai-may bundle on his back, held by a cord around his neck. He rode throughout the camp and forbade all quarreling, foolish conduct, or raiding parties for the remaining days of the dance.

Following him was the chief of the warrior society policing this Sun Dance. After 1838 the Tai-may keeper rotated this responsibility among the five warrior societies. In earlier times either the Elks Band of warriors or the Big Shields had performed this function.

Then the Tai-may keeper rode majestically out a short distance upon the prairie, slowly circled the entire village while all watched him, and returned to his starting point, dismounted, and entered his lodge. The ceremonies of the annual Sun Dance had officially begun.

Within a short time that morning the ceremonial "Search for the Sacred Tree" commenced. Two young men, selected from one of the warrior societies, were conducted to the Sweat Lodge. Facing east, this lodge made of willow branches and covered with buffalo robes was called the "Holiest of Holies." To the side of the entrance was a firepit where the stones were heated. The ten Tah'-loup* medicine bundles, followed by the Buffalo Medicine Cult men, were brought from the keeper's tipi to the sweathouse and placed upon sagebrush. The heated rocks were put in the center of the lodge. Water poured over the heated

Kiowa Sun Dance, Summer 1874 (Keah-ko calendar). Celebrating his release from prison, White Bear gave his medicine arrow to White Cowbird. By this act, White Bear passed the leadership of the Koitsenko to White Cowbird.

*Tah'-loup is the plural for Tah'-lee.

Kiowa Sun Dance, Summer 1875 (Keah-ko calendar). This Sun Dance became known as the "Love-making Sun Dance" because some young braves stole two Kiowa girls.

Kiowa Sun Dance, Summer 1876 (Keah-ko calendar). Some Mexicans stole Sun Boy's horses at this Sweetwater Creek Sun Dance.

rocks produced steam which the Tai-may priest fanned while praying for good health, long life, success on the warpath, and other requests by the people. After praying four times, the priest covered the ten medicine bundles with scalps, including some newly acquired ones offered by warriors at this time.

After the two young men in the Sweat Lodge had endured at length the heat from the fires, boiling water, and hot rocks, the Tai-may keeper declared them sufficiently purified for their task. They then began their search for the Sacred Tree. They preferred to search in the early morning, for they were forbidden to drink or sprinkle themselves with water during the hot mid-summer search. To drink or wash was a bad omen, suggesting rain which would spoil the Sun Dance.

The two young men cautiously searched for a strong straight cottonwood tree with a Y-shaped fork. A good stream of water and small green timber should be at hand. Room for all the campsites, including a good location for the medicine lodge, must also be nearby.

When the two scouts found a tree and site fulfilling all the requirements, they reported to the Tai-may keeper and were given water. The keeper called in the five bands of soldiers, four mounted groups and the fifth company of "Rattle" or foot soldiers, and announced the finding of the Sacred Tree.

The Rattle warriors remained to guard the camp while the Tai-may keeper with his sacred bundle led other medicine men and the tribe to the new campsite. The four bands of mounted warriors followed, and last came the women and children. Four times the tribe halted, and all those on horseback dismounted while the Tai-may keeper smoked a pipeful of tobacco. After the fourth pipeful, he extended his arm and pointed to the tree. All the young men raced forward, charging the tree as if it were an enemy. The first four to strike the tree could count coup.

In certain years the search for the Sacred Tree was held on the third day. Even so, the tribe still selected and occupied the campsite on the first day. A stake was planted at the location of the new campsite, and a race was held for two young men to count coup, the first by touching the stake and the second by running over it if he had previously run over an enemy in combat.

All then hurried to set up their lodges at the new campsite where the dance was to be held. The camp police carefully supervised the campsite so that the lodge circle provided an opening to the east and a large open space in the center for the medicine lodge.

Although other people have diagrammed the Kiowa Sun Dance circle, the accompanying plan is offered. Entering at the eastern opening and going counterclockwise, or south, the order of the bands was as follows:

Group 1 This largest division of Kiowas was known as the *Kátá*, or "Biters," a word that comes from the Arikara tribe. This old

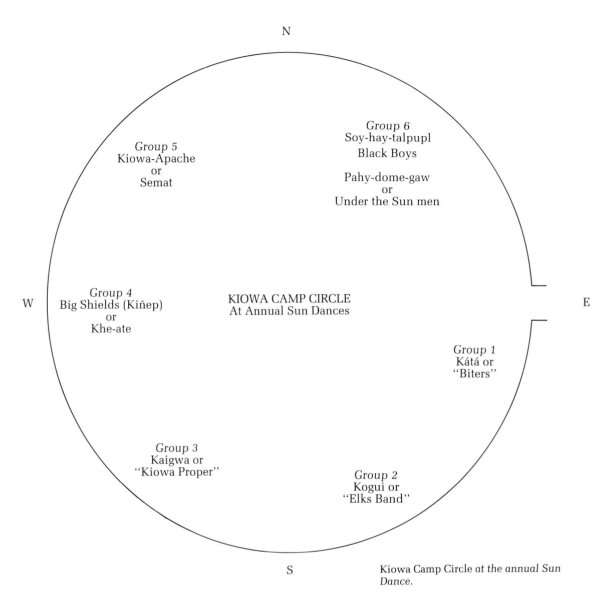

Kiowa Camp Circle *at the annual Sun Dance.*

Dohasan group occupies first place in the circle and held the hereditary right (duty) to furnish the buffalo for the Sun Dance. This group possessed many horses, tipis, etc.

Group 2 The *Kogui,* or "Elks Band," was noted for leadership in war ceremonies. It had many war families dating from Ad-da-te (1833) to Satanta, Big Bow, and others of the 1870s. The band boasted warriors with many military citations and recognized war deeds and coups. This group performed the war ceremonies at the Sun Dance.

Group 3 The *Kaigwa,* or "Kiowa Proper," commanded the respect of all other groups because it kept the sacred idol, the Tai-may. This small group was prestigious.

Group 4 The *Kiñep,* or "Big Shields," group was sometimes called the Sun Dance Shields. This group policed the Sun Dance. The group might more appropriately be called by their Kiowa name: *Khe-ate* (*Khe* = shield; *ate* = large).

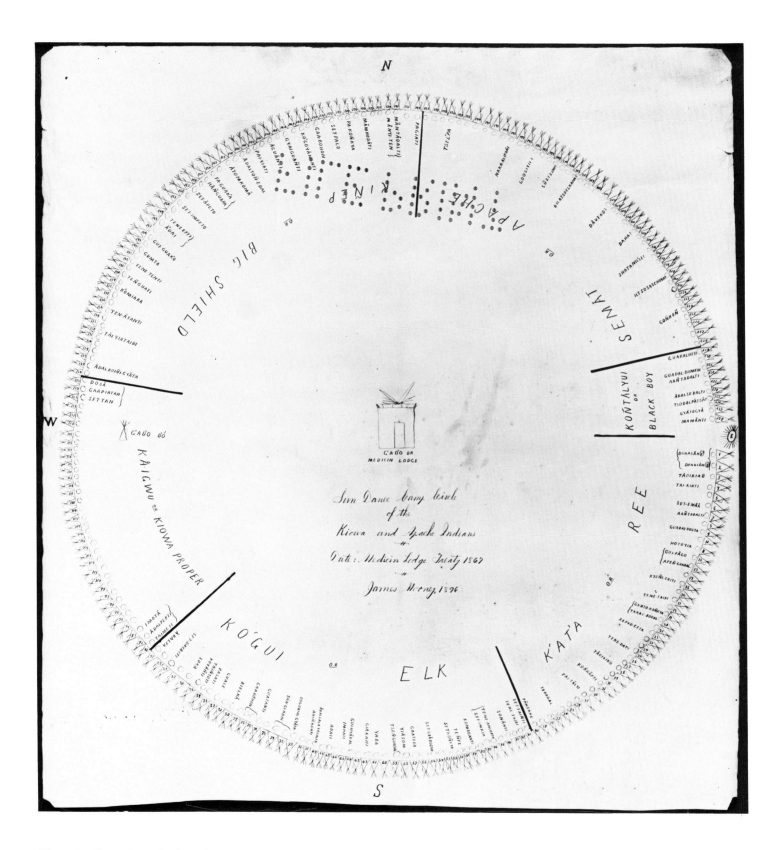

Kiowa Sun Dance Camp Circle at the
Medicine Lodge Treaty, 1867, including
the Kiowa-Apaches. Chart prepared by
James Mooney. 1896.
Courtesy Smithsonian Institution.

Group 5 The *Semat*, or "Thieves," was another name used by the Kiowas in reference to the affiliated Kiowa-Apaches. This group was a distinct tribe and did not belong to the Kiowa political subdivisions proper. They were, however, allowed to be a part of the tribal circle.

Group 6 The *Soy-hay-talpupl*, or "Blue Boys" group has sometimes been called Sindiyuis or Saynday's people — a name taken from the mythical culture hero. This political group is Kiowa and sometimes has been erroneously divided into two groups. Also called the Montalyui, or "Black Boys," the band is known to the tribal elders as the *Pahy-dome-gaw* (Under the Sun men).

At one time there had been a seventh band, the Kuáto, or "Pulling Out" group, which separated from the main body of Kiowas on the northern Plains. The Kuáto may have been the unidentified group exterminated by the Dakota Sioux around 1780 as recorded in Dakota legends.

Each of the surviving six bands had its own chief and was subject to his leadership. Some also had their own religious medicine or ceremonial cults, but for the tribal gathering at the annual Sun Dance each band had a designated segment of the circle.

The camp circle symbolized the sun or moon. It also had the fortunate aspect of eliminating the "head" or "foot" concept, thereby preserving the pride of all bands.[6]

THE SECOND "GETTING READY" DAY

On the morning of the second day a seasoned warrior from the Biters' Band, which enjoyed the hereditary honor to kill the buffalo bull for the ceremony, prepared for the hunt. His wife accompanied him and aided him in the necessary rites. During the hunt neither the warrior nor his wife could eat or drink.

The Tai-may keeper presented the warrior with two arrows, though the Kiowas expected him to kill the bull with a single arrow to the heart to prevent excessive bleeding. A bloody kill, requiring both arrows, was a bad omen indicating that great sickness would come to the Kiowas. These beliefs were held in later days when only a single rifle shot was expected for the kill. Before releasing his arrow, the warrior counted all his coups. After shooting the buffalo, he forced the bull to make its death run. When dying, a buffalo bull usually faces eastward and collapses upright on its belly. If the animal died in this manner, it was a good sun sign.[7]

After the buffalo's death, the hunter and his wife followed a strict ritual:

Kiowa Sun Dance, Summer 1878 (*Keah-ko calendar*). *One of the two occasions in Kiowa history when the tribe held two Sun Dances the same year. Note the two altar poles which indicate a repeated Sun Dance.*

1. They picketed their horses facing south.
2. They bundled sage grass and brought it to the bull.
3. They put dried chips about 15 feet west of the bull and spread sage upon the chips.
4. The hunter recited his most famous coup.

Completing this ritual, he and his wife removed a wide strip of hide extending from the buffalo's tail to, and including, the head. The hide was rolled up to the head and placed together with the sage and chips upon the warrior's horse, which was now turned to face east. The warrior then offered a prayer to the sun:

> Sun, look at me.
> Let our women and children multiply,
> Let buffalo cover the earth,
> Let sickness disappear.[8]

Mounting his horse, he turned to the left and trotted back to the village with his cargo. His wife followed on her horse.

As the hunter rode to camp, he stopped four times before reaching the Tai-may keeper's lodge. The Kiowas' greatest chief, dressed in his ceremonial regalia, met the rider at the lodge and received the buffalo hide. As the chief placed the hide with its sage and chips on the ground, women and children came forward to attach presents to the hide while singing the Kiowa Prayer to the Sun:

> Sun, let us all live a long life,
> Sun, let us all live a long life.

The greatest chief was now joined by another chief. Moving in single file with their backs to the east, they carried the buffalo hide to the sweat lodge for purification rites. The Tai-may keeper and a few selected men followed. Seven times they put water on the hot stones, opened the door, and closed it again while offering prayers to the sun. The two chiefs then carried out the buffalo head and skin, halting four times in their return to the Tai-may lodge.

THE THIRD "GETTING READY" DAY

At mid-morning of the third day of the Sun Dance ceremony, the Sham Battle or "Laugh Fight" was held. The Kiowa warriors were dressed in their ceremonial eagle feathers and warbonnets and carried shields, guns, or spears.

The Rattles, or foot soldiers, stationed themselves in the center of the camp. The four bands of mounted warriors went a distance from the camp and came galloping through the east opening. They circled the camp, going counterclockwise, and rode out again. They did this four

Buffalo Head and Hide for Sun Dance *which would be placed in the "Y" of the altar pole in the medicine lodge. Courtesy Richard Pemberton.*

times.

The foot soldiers then made a brush fort around the Sacred Tree and formed a defense line behind the brush. The mounted warriors charged up in a cloud of dust, "play shooting" their empty guns and throwing their spears, while the defending foot soldiers retreated inside their brush fort. After more "shooting" and whooping, the Rattles "surrendered" and the Sham Battle ended. The Sacred Tree had been "won" by the tribe for the next event.

The time had arrived to chop down the Sacred Tree so that the tribe would have the forked center pole for the Sun Dance lodge. A captive woman with her face painted yellow approached the chosen tree. The tribe called her *Skow-tow-mah* (Medicine Bank Woman), for she always chopped the tree down and cut off its branches. If she erred in the ritual of cutting and was struck dead by the spirit force, at least a native Kiowa would not be lost. She trimmed the tree and left only the pole with its Y-shaped fork at the top. At the bottom she painted four red stripes.

A selected mounted warrior then rode up and honored a woman of his choice by inviting her to ride with him. Then stopping four times on the way, he triumphantly pulled the great pole to the center of the camp.

Meanwhile the *Sai'hee-tsow-hee*, or Calf Old Woman Society, had dug a hole for the center pole. A chief stepped forward and put it upright in the hole. This forked center pole served as the altar for the Sun Dance lodge, and it had to be strong to bear weight. The Kiowas called it the Altar Pole (religious term), or the "Boss" Pole (construction term), for it stood eighteen to twenty feet in the air and dwarfed the other poles of the medicine lodge.[9]

The altar pole had special power and often during the ceremonies gave its powers to medicine men to cure illnesses. The presence of the spirit force of the medicine lodgepole has manifested itself many times. Living tribal elders recall the following miracle.

Altar Pole Spirit Force

ONCE DURING A SUN DANCE IN Montana, a little child who was dying was brought into the medicine lodge. The child's father implored a 94-year-old Cheyenne medicine man sitting in the southwest corner of the lodge to smoke and pray for the child. The medicine man asked for a red hot coal to be placed next to the altar. He took some incense, went to the altar pole, picked up the live coal with his bare hands and rubbed it between his palms. Then he

Kiowa "Sham Battle" *at the Sun Dance ceremony. This nineteenth-century painting on cowhide depicts the "battle" for the Sacred Tree, which the Kiowas would later cut down to provide the center pole for the Sun Dance medicine lodge. Courtesy Smithsonian Institution.*

touched the incense and laid his hands on the body of the child. Next, he blew four times on his eagle-bone whistle; then he went to the dry altar pole and, as if by magic, he sucked water from it and sprayed it upon the child. The child responded immediately and became well. The pole and the old man possessed a power. His eagle-bone whistle was later given to a Kiowa, the keeper of one of the ten Tah'-loup medicine bundles.[10]

AFTER THE CENTER POLE WAS ERECTED, THE Calf Old Woman Society danced. For many years the Kiowas had two women's societies. The Calf Old Woman Society granted membership only by invitation to elderly grandmothers who had given at least four public feasts. The other female society, known as the *Sate-tsow-hee* or Bear Woman Society, was a religious society so secretive that most Kiowas feared its members. The extent to which these strong young women participated in the Sun Dance ceremonies remains unknown today.

As soon as the Calf Old Woman Society had completed its dancing, the Tai-may keeper circulated the great Straight Pipe, so-called because it had a straight tubular bowl in line with the stem. It belonged to the tribe prior to the earliest tribal memory. With the smoking of the ancient pipe, the rituals for the third day of preparation ended.[11]

Kiowa Eagle-bone Whistle. *This whistle, made from an eagle's wing, was used by a Crow medicine man the last thirty-three times the tribe performed the Sun Dance. His grandson then presented it to the son of a Kiowa Buffalo Medicine Cult member.*
Courtesy Linn Pauahty.

THE FOURTH "GETTING READY" DAY

The medicine lodge floor plan was laid out on the fourth day. Originally twenty-eight but in later times only seventeen forked cottonwood poles were cut and placed on the outer perimeter equidistant from one another, forming a circle of sixty to seventy feet in diameter. Each perimeter pole, twelve to fifteen feet high, was connected to the center pole by other cottonwood poles laid horizontally in the forks and tied with rawhide ropes.

Cedar branches and small cottonwood limbs were then cut and brought to camp for completion of the lodge. While cutting the poles and branches, the people were scattered throughout the woods, laughing and singing. This was the occasion for courtship, and the young were not chaperoned. Sometimes older men were later called to account publicly for their misbehavior during the Sun Dance ceremonies.

THE FIFTH "GETTING READY" DAY

The fifth day the Kiowas built the walls of the lodge and placed the small cottonwood and cedar branches on the top edges of the roof poles, thereby covering one-third to one-half of the lodge from the edge toward the center pole. Then they placed cedar poles and branches inside the lodge to form a long screen. The Calf Old Woman Society and the young boys of the Rabbit Society brought clean white sand from the nearby river. They covered the entire lodge floor with the sand, piling a cone two feet high around the base of the center pole. Each morning thereafter their job was to clean and smooth the sand. Their last act in the day's ritual was to place a large flat stone in the doorway of the lodge. Whenever a dancer entered or left the lodge, he stepped on the stone to prevent bad luck from descending upon him.

When the construction of the lodge was completed, the warrior societies held a celebration. Everyone, including drummers and dancers, took part in the festivities. During the rejoicing, the Sun Dance shields were hung and last minute decorations in the medicine lodge were completed. If weather conditions had earlier prevented the "Sham Battle" for the Sacred Tree pole, the tribe now held the ritual for the Sacred Tree lodge.

THE SIXTH "GETTING READY" DAY

Early in the morning of the sixth "getting ready" day the comical "Mud Head" ceremony was held. Men acting as "Mud Heads" or clowns rushed playfully through the camp, taking anything left outside the lodges. Mud-coated buckskin masks hid their identity, and they

Construction of the Sun Dance Lodge, Part I.
Adapted from Marriott, Saynday's People (1963).

Construction of the Sun Dance Lodge, Part II.
Adapted from Marriott, Saynday's People (1963).

played tricks on anyone they could catch. If no one was available, the clowns pretended to be others and acted out jokes on tribal members. One benefit of the expected arrival of the Mud Heads was that the lodge area was kept clean.

Following the comic rite of the "Mud Heads" came the serious ceremony of "Herding the Buffalo," a ritual and prayer for successful hunts. About fifty men and boys and one woman dressed in buffalo hides. The same woman always accompanied the men, for it was her office or prerogative; the Kiowas called it her "road of honor." Moving out to the prairie, these celebrants imitated buffaloes by playfully butting and kicking one another before standing still or lying down on the grass.

In camp a selected man wearing a special necklace stepped out of his lodge. He carried a bow and quiver with arrows in his left hand, and he held a firebrand in his right. Going to the medicine lodge, he sat down and talked with the Tai-may keeper about the "buffaloes" on the prairie. Soon he arose, trotted out with the firebrand, and sneaked upon the human buffaloes from the windward side. When the "buffaloes" smelled the smoke of the burning firebrand, they arose and ran from him.

The Tai-may keeper now appeared at the door of the medicine lodge. A Buffalo Medicine Cult man with the great Straight Pipe stood in front of the lodge facing the "buffaloes." Four times he pointed his pipe at them with his left hand, and each time as he withdrew the pipe he returned to the medicine lodge door. As he puffed smoke toward the four corners of the earth — east, south, west, and north — and finally toward the sun that gave the Kiowas light, he uttered his prayer:

Kiowa Sun Shield *given to James Mooney about 1895. The shield bears the sun emblem. Eight Sun Dance shields were hung on the cedar curtain in the medicine lodge.*
Courtesy Smithsonian Institution.

> *O Dom-oye-alm-daw-k'hee, creator of the earth,*
> *Bless my prayer and heal our land,*
> *Increase our food, the buffalo power,*
> *Multiply my people, prolong their lives on earth,*
> *Protect us from troubles and sickness,*
> *That happiness and joy may be ours in life.*
> *The life that we live is so uncertain,*
> *Consider my supplications with kindness,*
> *For I talk to you as yet living for my people.*[12]

After the pipe ceremony, the Tai-may keeper withdrew into the lodge, seated himself on the west side by the shields, and waited.

The "buffaloes" on the prairie were drawn to the lodge by the symbolic gestures of the pipe man. Four times they circled the medicine lodge counterclockwise before entering. Once inside, they ran around the center pole four times and then lay down.

The man with the firebrand was called "The Man Who Drives the Buffalo." The one with the Straight Pipe was called "The Man Who Brings the Buffalo." They and the other Buffalo Medicine Cult men, all wearing buffalo robes, sat down with the "buffaloes" while the entire tribe watched.

Three additional men then entered, each holding a straight pipe supplied by the Tai-may keeper. The pipes with black stone bowls and wooden stems were very old; Kiowa tradition says that they, together with the larger Straight Pipe, had always belonged with the Tai-may. Two of the three men searched under the robes that the "buffaloes" were wearing until they found a warrior who had counted many coups. When he was located, the third man touched him with his straight pipe and loudly called his name in honor. The entire tribe cheered and clapped. This ceremony was repeated four times to honor the four greatest Kiowa chiefs who had struck their enemies the greatest number of times during the past year.

After the ceremony everyone went outside and waited for sundown. In the meantime and in accordance with ritual, the medicine lodge keeper took the Tai-may doll from its pouch and carefully unwrapped it. After decorating it with feathers, he tied it on the end of a six-foot pole and again covered it. To mishandle this ritual meant that death would come to the keeper. Tribal elders still speak of the seriousness of this rite and have given this account:

Medicine Lodge Ritual

THE KEEPER OF THE KIOWA MEDICINE lodge during the Sun Dance was Loki Mo-keen, a Mexican captive taken as a small child. His Kiowa captor offered him to the Tai-may at a Sun Dance. When Mo-keen became of age, he exercised the ordained authority to unwrap the Tai-may and place it in the medicine lodge for ceremonial exposure. If any ritual rules were violated during the procedure, death would come to Mo-keen and not to a blood Kiowa. Mo-keen had faith in the Tai-may and served as the priestly keeper until his death in 1934. He lived to be more than a hundred years old.[13]

EVERY ACT OF THE KEEPER WAS WATCHED by his four assistants and the tribal medicine men. Upon completing the ritual, the keeper and the others in the lodge marched out exactly at sunset, singing their way to the Sun Dance lodge. Starting at the western side of the lodge and singing as they marched in single file, they circled it four times.

With the final circle the Tai-may keeper held the covered sacred image aloft while the people sang four songs. Then reentering the lodge, he placed the Tai-may to the left of the center lodgepole and in front of the cedar screen which extended across the lodge from north to south. Before the Utes captured the two smaller dolls in 1868, he also planted these images — one called "Man" and the other "Woman" — on either side of the larger doll; all the images faced east.   Three feet separated the cedar screen from the brush wall of the lodge where the dancers prepared themselves for the dance. Above the screen hung the eight Tai-may shields decorated with feathers and paint. Near the sacred medicine was a buffalo skull, painted red and black. The red half represented the attainment of old age, and the black half represented success in war. To one side of the medicine were two small hollow mounds, called censers, used for the burning of dried cedar leaves and branches to provide incense for purification.

The bottom of the center pole or altar was ornamented near the ground with the robes of buffalo calves, their heads facing up as if they were climbing the pole. The Y-fork at the top held cottonwood and willow limbs firmly bundled together and covered with the ceremonial buffalo robe, complete with head and horns, thereby forming the rude image of a buffalo facing east. The branches above the fork were similarly ornamented with colorful shawls, strips of calico, scarves, and feathers. The most colorful ornaments adorned the ends of the branches, while a black cloth covered the top.

In the procession led by the keeper were those men who would attempt to dance for four days without food and water. Usually there were many fasting family dancers in the beginning, but only a few by the fourth day because most dancers could not endure the rigorous ceremony. Once a dancer left the dance, he could not reenter it. Everything had finally been made ready, and the time for dancing had arrived.[14]

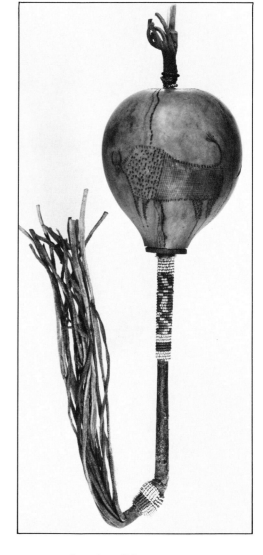

Kiowa Rattle *with Buffalo Power decoration. The rattle was used in Kiowa ceremonial dances in the nineteenth-century. Courtesy Smithsonian Institution.*

THE FOUR DANCING DAYS

The first of the four dancing days began after sunset, at the end of the "getting ready" days, and continued until midnight. The next three dancing days began at sunrise each morning and continued into the night, except for the last day, which ended at sunset. Each of the four dancing days, the Sun Dance Gourd keeper was in command of the Sun Dance participants and led them into the medicine lodge. First came the dancers and then the drummers-singers, who seated themselves on the ground near the entrance to the lodge. Usually the ceremonial drum measured three feet in diameter and accommodated ten drummers. At times rattles were also used. To one side of the drum a small fire was kept burning to tighten the rawhide drum head when it became slack.[15]

Normally the dancers were the Sun Dance Gourd keeper, his assistants, the shield owners, and the fasting family dancers, although med-

Four Dancers at Sun Dance. *This dance, held in 1933 on a Shoshone reservation at Fort Washakie, Wyoming, shows four dancers with the traditional barefeet, symbolic scalps hanging from the braids in the hair of two dancers, skirts hanging to the ankles, and all with eagle-bone whistles. Kiowas attended the ceremony but did not dance.*
Courtesy Susan Peters estate and Helen McCorpin.

Cloud Blower Pipes *were made from the leg bone of a deer and wrapped with sinew. These pipes were smoked skyward to draw well. Today's elders remember little about them. All are Kiowa pipes except the second one from the top which is Arapaho.*
Courtesy Smithsonian Institution.

icine men might join at times during the four days. The medicine men danced on behalf of family dancers who had planned to dance but had fallen ill.

The Sun Dance Gourd keeper, serving as mediator between his people and the sun, danced and fasted during the entire four days without leaving the lodge. His face, painted with red and black zig-zag lines running down from his eyes, resembled the Tai-may's face. His body was painted yellow; a blue or green design on his chest and back represented the sun. At times designs representing the moon were added, as was a long flowing human scalp fastened to his scalplock. He wore a long yellow deerskin skirt and a blue breechclout reaching to the ground. On his head was a jackrabbit skin cap with an eagle feather attached, and bands of sage hung from his wrists and ankles. He carried a piece of cedar in one hand an an eagle-bone whistle with a dangling eagle feather in the other. His feet were bare, as were the feet of all dancers.

The keeper had taught the sacred songs and ceremonial rituals to the four assistant dancers so that one of them could lead the dance in the event of an accident to the keeper. Each one served for four successive ceremonies, at which time their successors were chosen.

The assistants painted their bodies white or yellow and wore either long yellow or white buckskin skirts with breechclouts hanging outside in both front and back. Painted in the center of their chests was a round spot, representing the sun, flanked by two crescent moons on either side of the sun. This same design was duplicated on their backs. Scalps with eagle feathers hung from the braids in their hair. The head decoration was either a jackrabbit skin cap with an eagle feather attached or a wreath of sage. Their faces were painted with stripes across the foreheads which ran down the sides of their cheeks to meet across their chins. The assistants also wore sage around their wrists and ankles and carried pieces of live cedar and eagle-bone whistles. The assistants were responsible for all ceremonial painting.

Tai-may shield owners who danced with the keeper's assistants sometimes were painted with yellow or green designs representing the moon and sun. The remainder of their regalia resembled that of the fasting family dancers.

The faces, arms, and torsos of the fasting dancers were painted white. They wore white-painted buckskin skirts and blue breechclouts which hung to the ground, both front and back. Although bareheaded, they often wore sage tucked in at their waists. Like the other dancers, they had eagle-bone whistles. In later years these dancers also wore sagebrush wreaths around their heads and buckskin skirts or shawls about their waists, and they painted the upper parts of their bodies in various colors. The medicine men who danced were also painted white, wore white buckskin skirts with breechclouts outside, and carried eagle-bone whistles.

All of the dancers came from behind the cedar screen and sat facing the Tai-may. As the ceremony began, the dancers blew on their eagle-bone whistles, keeping time with the drums. When they rose to dance, they stood in rows facing the Tai-may. Standing fixed with knees bent, they slowly raised themselves upon their toes in time with the music and extended their arms toward the sacred medicine. Even as they moved about the dance area, they continued to dance with these movements throughout the evening.

At midnight the drummers and spectators went to their tipis to sleep. The dancers and the keeper remained in the lodge to rest. The only other relief the dancers had was the use of water lilies to cool their bodies, an act which carried a blessing with it. In later years the dancers were allowed to receive some nourishment from cattail roots, an ancient food traditionally used in other religious rites.

Activities daily resumed at the moment of sunrise, when the drummers returned and continued the music until the sun had risen. Following this sunrise service, the fasting dancers returned to the medicine lodge for the ceremonial smoke and prayer by the priest. Each family dancer received a sponge bath and then was painted anew. The artist chosen by the family painted the symbol of his own guardian spirit on the dancer's body. In appreciation the family presented the painter with a horse or a blanket.

Drummers, singers, and participants returned at noon. Dancing resumed again until sundown, when they stopped to smoke before resuming again in the evening and continuing until midnight. Others relieved them and danced until sunrise.

The Sun Dance Gourd keeper was always in charge of dancing events, but activities varied slightly each year. Individual dancers performed rather freely, and were permitted to rest behind the screen or at the edge of the arena.[16]

One of the major events of the second dancing day occurred when a middle-aged man, wearing a buffalo robe, came out to the center of the lodge and symbolically relived the death of the buffalo at the end of the hunt. He fixed his eyes on the sun and gazed at length. He began to dance slowly, then faster until his entire body vibrated from his frantic movements. His robe fell off, leaving him clad only in a blue breech-clout. As sweat poured from his body, he ran and jumped around the enclosure with his eyes still fixed upon the sun. Dancing until he collapsed from exhaustion, he simulated the buffalo's death by falling upon his stomach with his head facing east.

At another time during the ceremony the keeper, after burning cedar leaves as incense, chewed some medicine root and spit upon the moving dancers. Then taking the ceremonial fan of long crow feathers from behind the Tai-may, he moved around the dancers, waving the fan successively in vertical, circular, and horizontal movements. He then chased the dancers around the center pole until he separated one, who,

Kiowa Sun Dance, Summer 1881 (Keah-ko calendar). This dance was called the "Hot Sun Dance" because of the unusually hot and dry summer.

Kiowa Sun Dance, Summer 1884 (Keah-ko calendar). A Sun Dance was not held this year because buffalo could not be found.

Kiowa Sun Dance, Summer 1887 *(Keah-ko calendar). The Oak Creek Sun Dance was the last Kiowa Sun Dance held by official permission.*

Kiowa Sun Dance by Sharron Ahtone Harjo *(Kiowa, 1971). The artist, Miss Indian America of 1965, has depicted the medicine lodge with the eight shields hanging on the cedar screen. The Tai-may is to the left of the center (altar) pole. Courtesy Indian Arts and Crafts Board, Southern Plains Indian Museum and Crafts Center, and the U.S. Department of the Interior.*

after repeated blows from the fan, fell unconscious. If the dancer was fortunate, he would experience a vision about which he could later speak. Dancers chosen for this ceremonial "kill" were expected to be rewarded with good health and a long life.

The ceremonial "feather-killing" act usually occurred once each afternoon, although in some years one of the assistant dancers wielded the fan and the ceremony occurred three times daily—once each in the morning, afternoon, and evening.

Toward the end of the four dancing days piles of clothing, blankets, and various wares were placed on or around the Tai-may and, with much cleansing by smoke, three men and their sponsors danced around the sacred medicine. The dancers continued until they were driven away by the keeper. Articles presented to the Tai-may were believed to receive special powers to protect their owners from evil.

Shortly before sunset on the fourth dancing day the Sun Dance ceremonies ended. The dancers were given medicinal water, a little at a time, and the Tai-may was packed away with proper ceremony. Clothes and other items were tied to the center lodgepole as sacrificial offerings. That night a huge social dance was held, and in the morning the camp circle was broken.[17]

Raiding parties were organized by leaders during the final evening, and by the next day they were prepared to set off on the glory road. During the coming year young braves would attempt to assert their manhood and the seasoned warriors would try to reconfirm their courage and honor.

Before departing on the raid, the participants would perform the Buffalo Dance in hopes of receiving strength and courage from the Buffalo Guardian Spirit. The Buffalo Dance was the Kiowa warriors' special dance.[18]

Spirit Horse by Woody Crumbo (1957).
The horse symbolized speed and power
to the Kiowas; its tracks led people to a
righteous life. The Kiowa mystical spirit
horse was a powerful "medicine horse"
which was never tamed.
Courtesy a private collection.

IV P'-HAW-GOON

The Buffalo Dance (Kiowa War Dance)

We rode on the wings of the spirit horse,
Our enemies fearfully heard the drumming hoofs,
The Buffalo Guardian Spirit assured our victory
As we raced over the plains to avenge wrongs.

— Lee Satepetaw[1]

THE KIOWA MALE HAS ALWAYS BEEN conscious of his personal image. A proud person who values his dignity, he is jealous of his honor and concerned about his reputation as a man of abilities. His status and reputation, his courage and honor, could be tested in former times by his participation in a war party. Since the Kiowas never fought among themselves, the war parties always contained an element of the unknown, the mysterious, the dangerous. In preparation for the test of war, Kiowa warriors held the *P'-haw-goon* or Buffalo Dance.

The P'-haw-goon is an original Kiowa dance. When the Kiowas began keeping calendars in 1833, the P'-haw-goon was already a part of their culture. This Buffalo Dance is not to be confused with one of a similar name, the Buffalo Medicine Cult Dance. These two dances differ in purpose. Whereas the Buffalo Medicine Cult Dance was the ceremony employed by medicine men to achieve cures of the wounded, the Buffalo Dance is *the* Kiowa War Dance.[2]

Other tribes have their buffalo dances, but their interpretation and purpose differ from that of the Kiowas. Historically, the Kiowa Buffalo Dance originated when the tribe discovered the buffalo's many uses. According to folk memory, the Kiowas were acquainted with the buffalo culture while still in the Yellowstone region before the horse culture developed. Exactly when the Kiowa horse culture arose remains a matter of dispute, but by 1682 it had begun. The purpose of the Buffalo Dance was to appease the Buffalo Guardian Spirit. The image of the buffalo symbolizes power. The legend of the captive Kiowa Medicine Woman, who ran from the Pawnees and was saved by the buffalo power, reinforced tribal belief in the Buffalo Guardian Spirit.

When a Kiowa warrior faced the prospect of war, therefore, he turned to the buffalo as an example of courage. Whenever two buffalo bulls fought, they often fought until one died. Anyone who witnessed the struggle could attest to the fighting spirit and courage, the strength and endurance, the sheer power of both bulls before one triumphed. Recognizing the buffalo as a source of power and valor, as well as of food and strength, Kiowa warriors organized the P'-haw-goon or Buffalo Dance to honor the buffalo as their guardian spirit and as a source of courage to face the enemy even unto death.

Kiowa war parties had a variety of purposes. As few as one or two men, or as many as twenty or thirty men, went on raiding parties for horses and other material prizes. But a party of a hundred or more warriors indicated a revenge party against an enemy. Since revenge parties required so many warriors, they were usually organized when the entire tribe was assembled for the annual Sun Dance. Immediately following the Sun Dance, when the ban against war parties was lifted, each avenger or leader organized his expedition. Both the revenge party and the raiding party performed the Buffalo Dance as an integral part of their preparation.

The dance could be held any time of the year, in the camp or on the plains. When the dance was held in camp on the night before the departure of a war party, it also served as a recruitment device. The leader often began the camp cry-call in his tipi, alerting the village of his intentions with the *Gua-dawgyah*, or travel song.

GOING ON A WAR PARTY
(Gua-dawgyah, or Travel Song)

Going away on a war party,
That is the only thing to do,
That is the only road (way)
For a young man to gain fame and honor.

— *Wolf-lying-down (Lone Wolf's son)*[3]

Those warriors who chose to accompany him on the war party joined him in his tipi. Women followed and joined the men in dancing. After an interval the leader took the group outside to a stretched buffalo hide and used it as a drum. Traditionally no instrument was used except the hide, but in later times a small drum was used. Today a regular hand drum is employed. Dancers surround the drummers, who signal the beginning of the *Gwoh-dawgyah*,* or War Departure (Travel) Songs.

One year as the Travel Song was sung at the end of the Wolf Creek Sun Dance, the tree tops returned the song. The tribe ascribed the mysterious phenomenon to the "spirits," but south of the campsite was a bluff hidden by the woods from which the sound may have been echoed back.[4]

No special dance costume has ever been required for the Buffalo Dance which followed, although some dancers today wear a headdress of buffalo skin and horns. Others hold the tip of a buffalo tail (or buffalo hair) in their hand, switching it as they dance. Head dancers sometimes

*The new spelling for Travel Songs, Gwa-daagya and Gua-dawgyah being other alternative spellings.

wear a buffalo robe tied around their waists.

The Buffalo Dance and its songs have a unique rhythm that differs from all other Kiowa dances. The drummer uses a straight down beat, and the dancers rhythmically move up and down on their heels, holding their arms to their sides. The dancers are seeking courage and power, bravery and strength. Some of the songs require the dancers to simulate battle maneuvers and shout war cries. Occasionally a dancer will raise his lance or tomahawk into the air. These dance songs build up courage for battle. The words of two war dance songs, one old and one modern, follow.

KIOWA BUFFALO (War) DANCE SONG

O, Great Father, give me power over my enemies.
Make them blind that I may kill them.
Help me to steal good horses;
Give me health and a long life.[5]

The elders consider the following war dance song an example of those used for modern pageants.

MODERN WAR DANCE

And as our story comes to a conflict,
And so my ancestors live again their battles,
And these battles have become a ritual.[6]

The Kiowas who seek the source of their roots inevitably move in the direction of the past, to ritual. The Kiowa poet N. Scott Momaday has remarked that with each passing year, as he returns to witness the tribal culture relived through dance and song, he understands better the meaning of formality *and* the formality of meaning in Kiowa culture.[7]

Kiowa Warrior Preparing for a Journey *by Wilson Ware (n.d.). The artist depicted the Kiowa warrior wearing Kiowa beadwork and buffalo horns. Holding his lance with feathers indicating two previous coups, he is concentrating on his forthcoming journey on the war path. Courtesy KHRS.*

V GOMDA-DAWGYAH

Wind Songs

> *I have but one love,*
> *And he is far away*
> *On the warpath*
> *My days are lonely and weary.*
>
> —*Tane-tone (Eagle Tail)*[1]

THE RAIDING PARTIES WERE OFTEN away from the tribal camp, sometimes for weeks and months at a time. The braves on the war path and the loved ones left behind in the lodges put their thoughts and feelings into song. Another distinctive type of Kiowa song was thereby created, the *Gomda Dawgyah* or Wind Song.

The Wind Song is a war song, more accurately defined as a song of the warpath, usually created and sung by someone at home who thought of the distant warrior.[2] As a mother hummed a lullaby to the child in her arms, she also sang to the absent son far away. A maiden, dreaming of her absent lover, sang of her longing for him. The lonely warrior, remembering the joys of home, similarly put his thoughts into song.[3]

The songs were called Wind Songs because they tell of loneliness, of longing on the open prairie where only the sweep of the wind broke the silence. The following examples suggest the variety within this mode.[4]

MAIDEN'S SONG

Idlers and cowards are here at home now,
Whenever they wish, they see their loved ones.
O idlers and cowards are here at home now,
O idlers and cowards are here at home now,
But the young man I love has gone to war, far away.
Weary, lonely, he longs for me.[5]

YOUNG WARRIOR'S SONG

You young men sitting there,
You have wealth and parents, relatives, friends.
But me, I am a poor and lonely boy.
I will remain here and go on another expedition,
I know how to sleep and eat on the prairie
*   away from home.*
This kind of life makes me happy and content.

Wind Song (Gomda-dawgyah) by Black-bear Bosin (1954). The single warrior has gone on a raiding party, possibly to obtain horses so that he can gain honor. As he wanders, he thinks of the tipi in the tribal camp and his loved ones left behind; he then sings a Wind Song.
Courtesy Philbrook Art Center.

LONELY MAIDEN'S SONG

When I see your parents and family,
My heart is filled with joy;
It is as if I saw you in person.
Why do you act hard to get?
I heard that you are not coming home,
But will leave again for another journey.

GRANDMOTHER'S SONG

It is difficult to challenge a warrior's experiences.
You put yourself always in the front line;
A good warrior risks his life to defend his people,
And he also hopes to win the beautiful maiden
    of his dreams.

LONELY WARRIOR'S SONG

You warriors, you have loved ones
    longing for you; you are fortunate!
You lovers, you have maidens
    longing for you; I have none!
Why are you so downcast?
Lift your hearts with song!

WARRIOR'S SONG

I yearn for one special maiden,
And when I sing, I always call her name,
But I hear that I have not been accepted.
Now I am embarrassed and ashamed to return home.

GRANDMOTHER'S SONG

The land is great;
When a man travels on it,
    he will never reach land's end.
But because there is a prize offered
    to test a man to go as far as he dares,
He goes because he wants to discover his limits.

MAIDEN'S SONG

I am thinking of you,
I have not forgotten you.
My heart was made glad,
When I thought you were coming home;
But I heard you turned back,
You decided to go on another expedition.

Lonely Warrior Singing his War Path
(Travel) Song, *adapted from Stephen
Mopope's "Ceremonial Drummer."
Courtesy the U.S. Department of the Inte-
rior, Southern Plains Indian Museum and
Crafts Center, Anadarko.*

Wind Spirit by Blackbear Bosin (1955).
Courtesy Philbrook Art Center.

The day eventually arrived, however, when the war party returned
from its expedition. Excitement spread through the camp as the returning warriors drew near. The grandmothers and young maidens anx-
iously awaited, hoping to learn of the party's success but fearing the
possible report of a warrior's death. Good news produced a happy
ceremonial warrior's dance, while bad news resulted in a song of
mourning.[6]

VI **AWL-DAW-GHOON-GAH**

The Scalp Dance

There was a time of victory,
The charge, the pole of hair, the dance.
There was the time of death,
The wound, the fall, the mourning.

—T'ow-hadle (Laura Pedrick)[1]

THE RETURN OF A SUCCESSFUL REVENGE party, or a raiding party that had taken a scalp, was an occasion for rejoicing among the Kiowas. The women honored the triumphant warriors by dancing the *Awl-daw-ghoon-gah**or Scalp Dance, also recognized as a victory dance. *Awl-Daw* means "hair," hence the name Scalp Dance because the triumphant warriors returned with enemy scalps. The dance may be almost as old as the Kiowa tribe itself. Kiowa tradition says the dance has existed since warfare began, and the Kiowa calendars are silent concerning its origin.[2]

If even one warrior in a Kiowa war party had been killed, however, no Scalp Dance was held but a Mourning Dance was enacted instead. All newly acquired enemy scalps were thrown away. The Song of the Beautiful Maiden recalls such an occasion. The young maiden had heard that the warriors were returning to camp after a battle. She waited expectantly for her lover, a member of the raiding party, to charge victoriously into camp. But the war party rode slowly into camp as the leader gave the signal of death. The young maiden's warrior had been killed in an encounter with the enemy. Her mourning song followed:

SONG OF A BEAUTIFUL MAIDEN
(War Path Song)

I ran to the brook to do my hair.
I painted my face with colors of the evening skies.
My aunt chose for me a bright blue shawl like the sky above,
But, instead, we heard "How-oh-yo, How-oh-yo,"
Which meant darkness to all my people.
I ran back to my tipi
And with my tears washed off the paint until none was seen.[3]

Under happier circumstances, the successful party with scalps and booty always stopped short of the village to dress in full ceremonial regalia and to blacken their faces as an indication they had slain an

**The Kiowa word gah means society; other preferred spellings are gha and gaw.*

enemy. Then the warriors charged into the village, firing guns and shooting arrows to simulate their attack on the enemy. Usually they returned early in the afternoon in order to provide enough time for the evening's Scalp Dance festivities.

Once in camp, each warrior lifted his woman on to his horse, circled the camp, and sang. The scalps, painted red on the inside, were stretched on hoops and held aloft by the women on six-foot poles to honor their returning warriors.

If time did not allow the dance festivities to begin the first night of their return, the painted scalps were carried in an evening processional led by the grandmothers or other elders of the tribe. For the remainder of the night the scalps were placed in a special tipi called the Lodge of the Old Men. To the tribal elders, the war party leader gave an account of the entire enterprise and elaborated on all acts of bravery or cowardice.[4]

Whether the dance began that evening or the next day, the ancient ritual was not limited to any particular season or time. It could be celebrated during any season of the year, whenever a war party was successful. In the old days the Scalp Dance often lasted longer than is now customary.[5]

A large drum with several singers has always been used for the Scalp Dance. Originally the scalps were placed on poles in an arena, where the women danced around them. A circle dance, the Kiowa Scalp Dance moves counterclockwise, unlike the circle dances of all other Plains Indians. In the past, women dancers seized the lances or spears of their men, danced in reverse-circle fashion around the war trophies, and made feints at scalps with the lances and spears to simulate the "kill" of the enemy. The Scalp Dance has always been an individualistic dance, thereby allowing each woman opportunity to improvise during the dance.

Today women participating in the Scalp Dance follow a dance pattern similar to that of their ancestors. They carry their men's ceremonial lances. Instead of scalps, the women attach to the lance such modern trophies as banners, medals, and other military awards earned by Kiowa sailors and soldiers serving in the U.S. armed forces in Europe, Asia, and other foreign lands.

On the northern Plains long ago, no costume was specified for the Kiowa women performing the Scalp Dance. About a hundred years ago on the southern Plains, however, the women began to wear their returning warriors' ceremonial war costumes, including warbonnets. Now women wear a uniform red shawl with white letters on the back. Many women today are members of the Kiowa War Mothers' Chapter, which has assumed most of the former grandmother functions. The organization is active and progressive, and its members also serve as hospital aids, organize and conduct charitable functions, and send letters and Christmas presents to Kiowa soldiers.[6]

Ceremonial Scalp Dancer. *This picture shows the wife of Maw-na-khee (Kiowa Bill) wearing her husband's ceremonial clothing for the Scalp Dance long ago. Courtesy Susan Peters estate and Helen McCorpin.*

Warrior with Enemy Scalp *by James Auchiah (1929). The returning victorious warrior placed the enemy scalp on the pole and recited his deeds to the assembled tribe. Courtesy Oklahoma State Historical Library.*

Some songs of the Scalp Dance contain vocables; others contain words. Those with words often suggest deeds and stories in honor of outstanding warriors. One popular song presupposes the following knowledge of Chief Lone Wolf's revenge war party.

In 1873 some troopers fought a Kiowa/Comanche war party near Fort Clark, Texas, and killed Lone Wolf's son and nephew, Tau-ankia and Guitan. Lone Wolf's revenge party encountered some Texans who fled, except for one who fought and died. The Kiowas discovered the Texan's repeating rifle fired eight bullets without reloading. Lone Wolf's Song recalls the event.[7]

LONE WOLF'S SONG

Just because he had eight bullets in his gun,
He felt safe.
But I see that he did not come home.[8]

The underlying story of another song tells of a Kiowa revenge party that flushed out the enemy. One of those fleeing from Kiowa warriors became entangled on a vine as he scrambled down a cliff. While hanging there, he begged for his life, promising his pursuers great rewards. They ignored his entreaties, killed him, and took his scalp. The song contains these words:

SCALP DANCE SONG

We are not concerned
Whether you are rich or poor
When you become our enemy.

We do not care
Whether you are rich or poor

And now you are hanging down;
You are pleading for your life.[9]

Kiowa singers also intersperse their Scalp Dance songs with the Death Songs sung by the Tiah-pah or the Black Legs celebrants. This development reflects the modern practice of the Kiowa women dancing with both societies on either Armed Forces Day (May 30) or Veteran's Day (November 11).

CHIEF WHITE BEAR'S SONG
(There Will Be a Time)

There will be a time,
(When my body will be somewhere).
No matter where my enemies may destroy me.

Do not mourn for me
Because I will not be alive to know it.

There will be a time,
When my body will lie somewhere on a battlefield;
And the wolves shall devour me.
But do not mourn for me.
Because I will not be alive to know it.[10]

When the dance was completed, the scalps were offered to one of the ten sacred medicine bags containing the most scalp hair; hence the offering was to part of the original half-boy of Kiowa legend, Zye-da Tah'-lee. When offering the scalps, they prayed for long life, for power to take other scalps, and for calamity to strike their enemies.

A SCALP DANCE PRAYER

O Zye-da Tah'-lee, give us power to get other scalps.
Zye-da Tah'-lee, give us long life and make us brave.
Keep our enemies blind and deaf,
So they cannot detect our stealthy approach.[11]

With this prayer, the women's part of the victory celebration ended.

Tau-ankia, son of Lone Wolf, who was killed on a raiding party by soldiers near Fort Clark, Texas, in 1873. His cousin Guitan tried to rescue him and was also killed. Photo by William S. Soule, 1867. Courtesy Smithsonian Institution.

Women Scalp Dancers by Spencer Asah (1928). The two women carry their husbands' ceremonial lances as they begin the Scalp Dance.
Courtesy University of Oklahoma Museum of Art.

VII OHOMA

The Warrior's Dance

The eagle is majestic; the eagle is power.
The eagle holds the Voice of Thunder in its talons.
Circling above the plains and mountains,
Free, powerful, it commands us to dance to the drum.

—Linn Pauahty[1]

THE WARRIOR'S DANCE IS AN OLD dance of the Plains tribes. Oral tradition says the dance was given by the Northern Cheyennes to the Kiowas as a gesture of peace more than a hundred years ago. The Cheyennes, however, had received the dance originally from the Northern Omaha tribe, hence the Kiowa corruption of the name "Ohoma" for their lodge which preserves the dance.

Contrary to popular opinion, the Warrior's Dance was performed *after*, not before, a war expedition as a part of the larger victory dance or celebration. Through the dance, the braves reenacted in pantomime their battle deeds and other stories. Originally the dance was not associated with any special time of year, nor was there any particular number of dancers, although today it is one of the traditional summer dances.[2]

The Ohoma Society formerly was governed by a council of Kiowa war chiefs during the great days when the Kiowas roamed freely on the Plains. The council made decisions about festivities, "honor dances" for individuals and groups, mourning ceremonies for deceased members, and selection of the two appointed Head Dancers who wore the ceremonial bustles. With the beginning of reservation days, the Council of Chiefs evaluated the qualifications of anyone being considered for societal membership, and they placed emphasis on ancestral integrity since a new member was "being put instead of" his ancestor.

As late as the 1920s the Ohoma lodge was more active than the Tiahpah, but not today. The old Ohoma war chiefs originally in the lodge are dead, and leadership honor is now hereditary. If the society should be revived, the chief headsman would be Marland Aitson, the grandson of White Buffalo (Konad), the deceased hereditary keeper of the Ohoma drum, as agreed upon by surviving members in Oklahoma City, November 1, 1980. There is no longer a Council of Chiefs to make the dance decisions, but in July the members hold the annual feast and dance west of Anadarko.[3]

The dance ritual follows a regular routine which may consume half a day for each dance. For the Warrior's Dance, the Kiowas prepare an arena which is not necessarily circular but always faces east. Special

Ohoma Dancer by Jack Hokeah.
Courtesy KHRS.

singers gather at the edge of the arena and divide into two groups, corresponding to the membership of the Ohoma Lodge. The eagles sit on the south, or right side, while the Crows sit on the north, or left side. No difference in social distinction or status is implied by the location of the two groups, and both participate in the Charging Song conducted later in the ceremony.

The three ceremonial leaders today are the Headsman and the two official Head Dancers. The Headsman is in charge of the arena and directs all the rituals involved in the ceremonials. He informs the drummers and singers what songs will be sung and when they will be performed. The two official dancers, the only ones permitted to wear bustles or "tail feathers," are responsible for the special Ceremonial Dance and Feast.

Following an ancient Cheyenne tradition, the Kiowas always select two women from aristocratic Kiowa families and permit them to occupy positions of honor during the men's dance. Called the Two Women Dancers, they stand in one designated place while swaying and keeping time to the rhythm of the drum. These women have no other function, but presumably the old Cheyenne tradition gave some type of special recognition to their women participants.

Prior to the ceremony, the official appears who holds the traditional office of Keeper of the Drum. Although he does not necessarily play the drum, as custodian he places the drum in the center of the arena. The Kiowas regard the ceremonial drum with reverence, for it is known as the "Voice of Thunder." Long ago many men held a stiff, dried buffalo hide stretched out among them and beat it with sticks, thereby making

Ohoma Society Ceremonial Tail-Feather Dancers (1920) from left to right: Charley Tsalote, once Headsman of the Kiowa Ohoma Society; Richard Pauahty, brother of Linn Pauahty; George Mopope, father of Stephen Mopope.
Courtesy Susan Peters estate and Helen McCorpin.

The Original Ohoma (Warrior's Dance) Singers *who received the dance from the Northern Cheyenne in the nineteenth century. Photo (1888) left to right: Enoch Smoky, Little Joe, White Buffalo, Red Buffalo, Silverhorn, Pauahty.*
Courtesy KHRS.

Kiowa "Stretched Hide" or "song hide" at Anadarko, Oklahoma (1960), was the original Kiowa term for a drum. Courtesy Sooner Magazine.

a deep thumping sound. The ancient Kiowa word for drum, therefore, means "stretched hide" or "song hide."[4]

The top sides of all Ohoma ceremonial drums have identical decorations. Against a blue sky background an eagle holds a lightning bolt in his talons to symbolize the Voice of Thunder. The drum is supported by four sacred sticks, and at the end of each stick is the carved head of a warrior wearing one eagle feather. The rhythm of the drum is an invitation, actually a command, to dance.

In former times when the drummers began the rhythmic beat, the Head Chief of the Kiowas arose and the dance was officially in progress. Today the Ohoma Head Dancers give the command to dance by standing in the arena and moving their right feet sideways. This form of dance command stands in sharp contrast to the Tiah-pah Whip Man's command with his whip.[5]

Traditionally the Warrior's Dance could have included any of the following songs in the order listed below:

> Opening Song
> Chief Song
> Appeasement Prayer
> Feast, or Kettle, Song
> Charging Song (part of Feast ceremony)
> Tail Feather, or Special Ritual, Song
> Give-away Song
> Mourning Song
> Battle Story Song
> Closing Song

All of the songs were not necessarily included in the Warrior's Dance ceremony. The appropriate ones for the occasion were chosen by the Council of War Chiefs and supervised by them.

The Opening Song included the following words:

> Honor the brave,
> Honor the courageous.
> Let this warrior stand alone as a tribute
>   to bravery and courage.
> Let this man lead the procession.
> Sing a song and sound the drum
>   while lesser hearts follow.
> Follow this brave warrior in a dance
>   proclaiming his heroism and valor.
> Honor a brave man.[6]

As in the past, the northern Plains tribes nearly always use words with the songs in the Warrior's Dance. By contrast, the southern Plains tribes seldom have words for most of their songs. Instead they use only "vocables" or "note words," whereby they express their feelings through syllabic sounds used at varying pitches similar to the white man's "do-re-mi-fa-so-la-ti-do."

Ohoma songs are sung at high pitches, reflecting the northern Plains influence; but the Kiowas sing at a slightly lower pitch than the Northern Cheyennes or Omahas. The tempo of both the Opening and the Chief Song is slow and dignified.

Following the Opening Song, the official Chief Song today still contains the original words:

> If you are a leader,
> Arise and dance.

With this summons, the war chiefs then led the warriors into the arena. In succession throughout the day the other chosen songs followed. Today the Opening Song and the Chief Song are the same, but the others may vary on an individual basis until the Closing Song, which always has contained the same ritualistic words.

There have always been two so-called Chief Songs in the Kiowa Ohoma dance, but the one given in the preceding paragraph traditionally was reserved for the Council of War Chiefs to sing following the Opening Song. The other could be sung by everyone elsewhere in the ceremony if they so desired. This pattern under the Ohoma Headsman apparently remains the practice today.

The Appeasement Prayer to the Earth-maker was not a regular feature in the ceremony. Only twice in the twentieth-century has it been offered, and only when the tribe prayed for calm and peaceful weather during storm conditions. The first time was in 1920 at Headsman Ed Keahbone's dance on Hog Creek, five miles west of Anadarko, Oklahoma. The second occasion was in 1923 at Headsman Jim Tongkeamhay's dance thirteen miles south of Carnegie.[7]

The Feast Song, often referred to as Kettle Song, contains only vocables or "note words." After singing this song, the Ohoma Lodge still preserves its ancient pattern of *encores*. In the Ohoma way of singing, the Leader gave the introductory words or vocables, the others picked up the song and tempo of the leader, and encores or seconds came at the conclusion. The Ohoma Lodge originated the practice of encores with the universal songs of the Plains tribes. The Ohoma song pattern of encores has powerfully influenced the song-dance ceremonials of all other Plains people, for they now follow the pattern of Kiowa encores.

As part of the Feast ceremony, the Charging Song suddenly revives the assembly. The two Ohoma groups, the Eagles and the Crows, perform the ritual of the "Sham Battle." The war chiefs tell the story of the victorious war expedition, and the two groups act out the battle. As they

Chief White Horse, *former leader of the Ohoma Society and the last of the original war chiefs of the Society.*
Courtesy Oklahoma State Historical Library.

Kiowa Flute Dancer *by Stephen Mopope. This dancer carries a flute in one hand and a fan of eagle feathers in the other. The dance is performed with the Ritual (Tail-Feather) Song.*
Courtesy Indian Arts and Crafts Board, the U.S. Department of the Interior.

Camp of Chief White Horse, 1893. *Photo
by Lanney.
Courtesy Smithsonian Institution.*

Fancy War Dancer by David Williams
(1967). This "Tail Feather" or "Ritual
Song" dancer wears the bustle (tail feathers) of a Chief Dancer and the roach
headdress of porcupine quills and eagle
feathers.
Courtesy Indian Arts and Crafts Board,
the U.S. Department of the Interior.

sing the "Charging Song," the sham battle takes place.

The Tail Feather, or Ritual Song, has always been highlighted by the spirited dancing of the Two Chief Dancers in their bustles or tail feathers. The feathers on the tail pieces are tied so that they fan out in a big circle like a sunflower. The dancers' head-dresses contain porcupine quills and eagle feathers. Since both dancers carry in one hand a flute with a Swift Hawk feather on its end, they have erroneously been called "flute dancers." They also carry in the other hand a fan of eagle tail feathers, from which the song has derived its name.

The traditional Give-away Song contains a gift presentation by one or more families to someone dear to them.[8] The Mourning Song, like the two previous and the following songs, contains only vocables. The dance movements and vocal tonality render mournful expressions and sounds for a deceased tribal member.

Following the "battle," each warrior tells his part in the victory and pantomimes his heroic feats in the Battle Story Song. As the song-dance temporarily stops, he approaches the drum in the center of the arena and briefly describes what he did and how it came to pass. Other warriors then follow him to the drum, individually dancing and telling their stories of bravery. In their songs of victory, the singers often repeat legend and lore, citing great deeds and calling anew for bravery and sacrifice. In these happy songs of victory, a wild exultation with little rhythm is sometimes evident. Today many songs are personal or family possessions containing war messages and war deeds of ancestors. After the individuals have told their stories, the ceremony closes with the ritualized Closing Song.[9]

The Warrior's Dance is fitting to the rich tradition of a brave and great tribe. Although the dance languishes today, perhaps the grandsons of the great Kiowa war chiefs will some day revive and revitalize the hereditary Council of Chiefs in the Ohoma Lodge.* Perhaps once again the Kiowas will take pride in the Warrior's Dance and the decisions of this council.

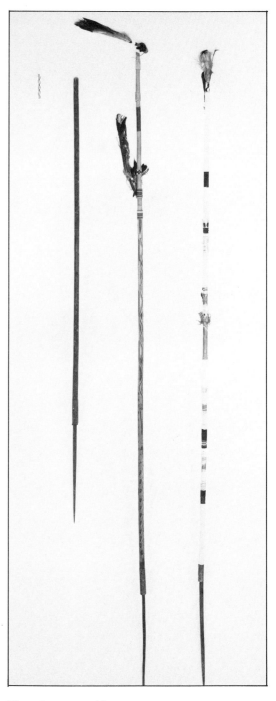

Kiowa Lances used by Kiowa warriors.
Courtesy Smithsonian Institution.

*In 1976 the surviving members of the hereditary council included Joe Poolaw, Mountain View; Walter Kokum, Saddle Mountain; Linn Pauahty, Lawton; Yale Spottedbird, Hobart; George Tsoodle, Mountain View; Mark Keahbone, Anadarko; Howard Geimahsaddle, and James Silverhorn.

VIII T'OW-KOW-GHAT

The Black Legs Dance

The force of life lay in the flesh wound,
  wedge-shaped, split, gaping;
The Black Legs spoke of courage and honor
  and death.
And what of Death and Time?
There is no death, only a change of worlds;
  and our world goes on!

   — T'ow-hadle (1925); Ha-Goon (c. 1887)[1]

DEATH HAS ALWAYS BEEN REGARDED with greater equanimity by the Kiowas than by the white man. Accepting death as a part of the order of the universe, the Kiowas see earthly life as consuming only a brief time before the individual spirit joins others in the land of the spirits. Formerly Kiowa warriors continuously exposed themselves to death as protectors of the tribe. The *T'ow-kow-ghat* or the Black Legs Dance and its songs celebrated both survival and honorable death.

One of the six original Kiowa warrior societies organized in 1838 after the great battle with the Cheyennes and Arapahos, the Black Legs Society was similar to the Tiah-pah Society and its inner group of Koitsenko, the Ohoma Society, and the Kiowa Warrior Gourd Clan. The leaders of the Black Legs Society carried a feathered lance resembling a shepherd's crook which was called Pa-bon, symbolizing the highest honor of the order. Chief Black Turtle was the earliest leader of the society, followed by Young Mustang, and then by Sitting Bear. White Bear, the leader of the Kiowa Warriors Gourd Clan, also held membership in the Black Legs Society.[2]

An early member of high honor in the Black Legs Society was Pawtawdle, called Poor Buffalo but more accurately translated as Lean Buffalo. Poor Buffalo established some of the concepts of bravery and honorable death for the Society, as verified by K'-hee-ale, or Big Man:

> During the battle the guns were firing fast. Men were falling on both sides. After a while I heard a warrior singing behind a rock pile. I stopped and looked. It was Poor Buffalo, one of the head leaders of the Black Legs Warrior Society. He was singing the Society's song. He said it was a greater honor to be killed by the enemy than to retreat, as this is the way of the great Koitsenko warriors.[3]

When a Black Legs leader was killed or died, another leader chosen from members of the organization was given the Pa-bon, or lance. If the leader became too old to carry the lance into battle, he gave it to a man of his choice. If the leader showed cowardice, the lance was taken from him and he was thereby dishonored. Sitting Bear (Satank) was the last actual war leader of the Black Legs Society. He forced his own death by rifle fire while a prisoner; he saw no hope of escaping with honor, so he chose death rather than humiliation in the white man's courts and prisons.

In early days a warrior belonging to the Tiah-pah Society did not hold membership in the Black Legs Society. Each Society required total loyalty, and a warrior could not serve both organizations. Today it is possible to belong to both societies, but most elders do not consider it good practice, and probably only a few Kiowas are members of both. Originally an exclusive society, the Black Legs remains today semi-exclusive. Formerly all members had to be Kiowas, and today all drummers still must be Kiowas. A few Comanches, however, recently have been inducted into the Society.

The Society derived its name from the members' practice of painting their legs black prior to a military encounter. This act was a mark of bravery in the face of death. The origin of the act has been disputed. Some say the original members were so brave that they often charged into the enemy's guns and returned to camp with black gunpowder on their legs.[4] Most tribal elders disclaim this story and insist that the following legend is true.

L ONG AGO A SMALL KIOWA war party encountered a larger enemy force. Recognizing that they were trapped, the Kiowa warriors hid in the brush and heavy grass of the prairie. Being afraid to attack someone they could not see, the enemy set the prairie on fire. The day wore into evening while the fire raged. The Kiowas could have run out and surrendered to the enemy, but they refused. Instead, they suffered the heat and slipped away after dark, walking and crawling through the hot, blackened prairie grass. They safely arrived at their camp the next day, but their legs were black as a result of the fire and charred grass.[5]

FROM THAT DAY, AS A MARK OF BRAVERY in the face of the

Pa-bon, Sash, and Lance Point *were part of some Kiowa warriors' ceremonial equipment in the nineteenth-century. Today the Pa-bon is featured in the Kiowa Gourd Clan ceremonials. Courtesy the Fort Sill Museum.*

Origin of the Black Legs

Black Legs Warrior *by Roland Whitehorse (1949). Courtesy Indian Arts and Crafts Board, the U.S. Department of the Interior.*

Satanta (White Bear). *Photo by William S. Soule (ca. 1870).*
Courtesy Bureau of Indian Affairs and the National Archives.

enemy, the Society dancers put ceremonial black paint on their legs. In later times, from 1910 through the 1930s, they wore black underwear-type leggings at camp gatherings. Today, they often wear black stockings or leggings, hence the modern term of Black Leggings Society is sometimes applied to the order.

In addition to the Black Leggings, the distinguishing symbols of the Society are the Sacred Arrow, the Red Cape, the Coup Stick, and the Roach Headdress.

The Sacred Arrow, actually the Pa-bon or lance, carries with it the old tradition that Poor Buffalo bestowed upon it powerful medicine before giving it to the father of White Bear (Satanta). As an early leader of the bravest Kiowa warriors, Poor Buffalo pledged in the name of his ten "Real Dogs," or Koitsenko, to lead every desperate charge and keep his place in the midst of battle until victory or death.

Poor Buffalo anchored himself to the ground by sticking the Sacred Arrow through his blue elkskin sash which encircled his neck like a collar. By dismounting during battle and plunging the Sacred Arrow through his sash into the ground, he was fixed in a standing position and had to fight in that spot until his war party was victorious or until, seeing that all was lost, his warriors gave him permission to retreat by riding over to him and pulling the Sacred Arrow from the ground.

If no one pulled the arrow out during their flight, the leader was duty bound to remain and die at his post. During the battle, he was obliged to remain stationary without attempting in any way to avoid danger. When Poor Buffalo eventually died on a pile of rocks during a battle, he

Satanta's Burial at Fort Sill. *James Auchiah, grandson of Satanta, carries Satanta's original ceremonial warbonnet on the horse's saddle at the reburial ceremony of Satanta in Chieftain Cemetery, Fort Sill on June 8, 1963. The original burial site was the prison cemetery at Huntsville, Texas, nearly ninety years earlier.*
Courtesy Jane Pattie.

Satank's Death Song *by Ernie Keahbone (1969).*
Courtesy Indian Arts and Crafts Board, the U.S. Department of the Interior.

was anchored to the Sacred Arrow. In so doing, he established a precedent for all future leaders of the Black Legs.

The ceremonial arrow was carried by leaders only when the war party anticipated a bitter fight. The leader could remain in camp and lend the arrow to another member who wished to distinguish himself in a war party, but only if a small foray was anticipated. Should the leader lend his arrow when a serious expedition was in preparation, he was marked as a coward and degraded from his rank.

The next symbol of the Black Legs Society, the Red Cape, has a tradition almost equally as old. The Red Cape became an early symbol of audacity, or bravery, because of the action of an early leader. Poor Buffalo's successor and the first official leader of the Black Legs was Skon-kee-kon-gia or Black Turtle,* a principal chief of the Kiowas who soon passed his leadership to Gool-ha-ee. The following story about Gool-ha-ee explains the symbolism of the Red Cape.

Kiowa Black Legs Dancers. These danc at Anadarko in 1968 are continuing the dancing traditions of an original men's warrior dancing society. The dancers wear red capes, roach headdresses, an shawls tied around their waists; they h lances and cover their legs in black. Courtesy Jane Pattie.

GOOL-HA-EE (YOUNG MUSTANG) was an extremely brave warrior who always lived up to the strict leadership requirements of the Society. Once when he was leading a war party, he encountered a Mexican army contingent. Noticing that the Mexican Commander was wearing a brilliant red cape, Young Mustang acted with surprising boldness. He rode up alone, jerked the red cape from the officer's shoulders, and killed him almost in the same gesture. The surprised Mexicans were thrown into confusion, and Young Mustang brought the red cape back to the Kiowa camp circle. It became a part of the symbolism of the Society.[6]

The Red Cape Episode

THE SYMBOLIC COUP STICK WAS ALSO significant for each individual member. The stick, called the "Badge of Empire," carried as many feathers on it as the warrior had coups.[7] Today it has as many feathers as its present owner has verifiable military missions, for instance, in World War II, Korea, or Vietnam.

The Roach Headdress is a ceremonial item worn at all dance gather-

*Skon-kee (black) kon-gia (turtle) has been referred to in white men's books as Pial-kon-gia which means "water bird" to the Kiowas.

ings. The elders, however, are uncertain as to either its origin or its symbolism.

Black Legs Society members are obligated to participate in their dances. Since this is a military organization, heretofore only men have danced, and they dress in a uniform costume. All wear a red cape, roach headdress, and a shawl tied around the waist. Usually rattles or bells are tied to their legs, which are painted or covered in black. Each dancer carries a coup stick, but the Sacred Arrow is carried by a dancing warrior only when he elects to tell his battle story to the tribe.

Originally the Black Legs Dance was not held at a specific time or season. Today it is annually presented at Indian City near Anadarko, Oklahoma, in May. The symbolical dance features military movements, battle scenes, and Charging Dance songs. The drum, beaten with a straight downward motion, suggests gunshot sounds. In one special sham battle dance, the dancers fire guns with blank shells to add realism.

Some of the most popular and revered songs of this ceremony are more than a hundred years old. Sitting Bear's Death Song is always included. Two versions are offered:

SITTING BEAR'S (Satank's) DEATH CHANTS

Even though I live now,
I will not live forever.
Only the Sun and the Earth
*   remain forever.*[8]

Oh Sun, you remain forever;
Oh Earth, you remain forever;
But we, the Koitsenko must
*   die!*[9]

Chief Big Meat's Death Song is also danced to and sung at every Society gathering.

BIG MEAT'S SONG

My warrior brothers (already dead)
Are calling me over there now.
I am getting ready to join them now.[10]

Another favorite song preserves the theme of the earlier death songs.

WHITE BEAR'S (Satanta's) SONG

No matter where I fall in battle,
Do not mourn for me.
For I will not know it.
Somewhere in some far off land
My body will be devoured by wolves.
But I will not know.[11]

Roach Headdress worn by Black Legs dancer. The origin and significance of the headdress has been lost in the tribal memory, but it is an ancient traditional part of the Kiowa warrior's costume. Courtesy Smithsonian Institution.

The Society still preserves Poor Buffalo's last wish of death with honor.

POOR BUFFALO'S SONG

All brave men must die sometime,
The Koitsenko must die, too:
It is a great honor to die in battle.[12]

On battlefields throughout the world in the twentieth century many Kiowas have fought and died without giving ground, as if the Sacred Arrow also held their sashes.

Satank (Sitting Bear) by William S. Soule (ca. 1870). Satank was killed May 28, 1871.
Courtesy Bureau of Indian Affairs and the National Archives.

IX **POLAH-YEE-GAH**

The Rabbit Dance

We are of one heart, the legends teach,
The line of life is clear, time is limitless,
The young seek roots, the reminders of the mind,
For they lead to the heart, to home.

— *T'ow-hadle (Limping Woman)*[1]

EVERY SOCIETY PROVIDES TRAINING for its young. The Kiowas are no exception. Apart from the white man's public school system, the Rabbit Order is the beginning of a clearly defined training ladder through which nearly all Kiowa youths pass. For the Kiowas, legend and ritual are intricately woven together. The legend of the Old Man and the Rabbits explains the origin of the Rabbit Order and the *Polah-yee-gah* or Rabbit Dance.

A Brave "Rabbit" *with the tools of the warrior.*
Courtesy KHRS.

The Legend of Grandpa Rabbit

LONG AGO OLD MAN BROKE THE LAWS of the Kiowa tribal council and was declared unfit to live with our people any longer. His punishment was exile. When the tribe moved to a new campsite, he was left behind.

That night sitting alone in the dark, Old Man became despondent. "My people have cast me out, so I shall die," he exclaimed.

He lay down to die. For a long time he was unconscious. Then one morning he was awakened by a multitude of rabbits.

"We care for you and will not let you die," they said. And so they hopped here and there, gathering food and water and shelter for Old Man.

Because of the rabbits, Old Man was encouraged to live. He stayed with them in the woods, learning their language and growing to love them. Aside from the rabbits and the village children in his former camp, he had never had any friends.

After Old Man had regained his strength, the rabbits suggested that he teach little boys how to become great men. Old Man pondered this idea for some time and then moved near the camp of his people.

He sent a message to all the young boys of the tribe to come to his place by the river. They came, and the first great meeting took place. Laws were passed, and Old Man was elected as the Head Rabbit. They originated their Rabbit Dance, patterned after the movements of rabbits, and composed their songs. Old Man received the name of "Grandpa Rabbit" and thereafter he taught little boys what they needed to know for manhood.[2]

When the tribal council learned about this new organization, they invited the Head Rabbit back to the village. His Rabbit Order was recognized and given an honorable place in the warrior orders. The Rabbits were designated to serve as official helpers in putting up the great ceremonial arbor for the annual Sun Dance. At the dance they also aided the Calf Old Woman Society in collecting and spreading the white sand for the floor of the medicine lodge.[3]

Young Rabbits in Training by Roland Whitehorse (1976). Young Kiowa boys, ages 8-12, learned to ride in preparation for later deeds of bravery.

NOW FOR A CENTURY OR MORE, NEARLY ALL Kiowa boys have been enrolled in the "Rabbits," the traditional first order in the male ladder of growth to manhood. Older men, called Leaders, teach them the skills needed for male success. The Rabbits learn to swim, run, hide, ride, shoot arrows, and throw lances. The traditional Kiowa orders for both young and old males are as follows:[4]

Age Group	Order
8-12	Rabbit
12-18	Young Sheep
Above 18	Warrior Society
	(One of six)

In former days when the young male adult passed through the two younger orders, he entered one of the six warrior societies. Of these six, only the Tiah-pah with its Koitsenko, the Black Legs Society, and the

Ray Doyah in Rabbit Dance costume. Courtesy KHRS.

The Rabbit Dance by Roland Whitehorse (1976). The "Rabbits" hold their hands to their heads above the ears, extend their first and second fingers upward, and hop in time to the song of the drum.
Courtesy a private collection.

possibly reviving Ohoma Society have survived. They still exist because each of the original members upon retirement or death could designate his hereditary replacement in the Order. The other warrior societies had membership requirements based upon coups earned from deeds performed on the war path, hunting buffaloes, or stealing enemy horses—deeds impossible to achieve after the disappearance of the buffalo and the beginning of the reservation period. As a result, these other societies have disappeared. Today young Rabbits can look forward only to membership in the Young Sheep, and then through family ties they may graduate into either the Tiah-pah, Black Legs, or Ohoma Society.[5]

In the past, Rabbits had their own little tipis and entertained themselves under the guidance of their leaders. Today at tribal dances they camp with parents and relatives, joining the other Rabbits in the morning for their special activities and dances. The Rabbits wear regular tribal costumes of buckskin shirts and leggings of a ceremonial nature, comparable to those of adult males.

The Rabbit Dance takes place after the Camp Parade in the regular dance circle or arena where the adult dances are held later in the day. A regular large drum, often with ten or twelve adult singers, is used for the Rabbit Dance. The Rabbits have their special dance, with words to songs which are exclusive to them.

By holding their hands to their heads above their ears and extending their first and second fingers, they create the illusion of rabbit heads and ears. As the drum beats, they keep their feet close together, bend their knees, and hop in time to the song. The Rabbit songs are sung in rhythmic time to blend with the motions of the young boys as they hop around. Rabbit songs are brief, playful, and educational.[6]

DANCE AND BE HAPPY

Dance and be happy,
Dance and be happy,
Let your ears wave back and forth,
*   And up and down,*
Because that is the way we Rabbits
*   dance.[7]*

Some Rabbit Songs, such as the following, teach social behavior.

THE COTTONTAIL AND THE JACKRABBIT

I came to the end of the mountain (the cottontail).
I met another kind of rabbit (the jackrabbit).
He showed his unfriendliness to me.[8]

The second stanza, which may be treated as a second song, describes the dress and physical characteristics of the cottontail and the jack-rabbit. The cottontail, according to the song, proudly wears buckskin with metal (silver) medallions on his leggings. The most noteworthy feature of the sloppily attired jackrabbit is his extra large stomach.

Following their morning dance, some grandmother usually provides oatmeal and milk for the Rabbits. Then a grandpa, or the Camp Leader, calls them out to clean up the camp. They are dancers, but not yet warriors.[9]

Jimmie Mamaday (Walking Alone) is a descendant of both Chief Lone Wolf I and Maman-ti, one of the most prominent of the Kiowa medicine men. He is the uncle of N. Scott Momaday. Jimmie is wearing typical Kiowa male apparel as a Rabbit: (1) shirt and leggings of yellow buckskin with white fringes; (2) beaver hair braids; (3) men's moccasins distinguished by flaps inside and fringes outside; (4) two beaded medallions sewn onto the fur; (5) frontal sash hanging from hips; (6) beaded sash of beans (Texas berries) over the shoulder running diagonally to the waist. Not visible in the rear of his head is a scalplock which is in the top rear center of his head—called the "third braid."
Courtesy Kiowa Historical and Research Society.

Not Yet a Warrior by Roland Whitehorse (1976).
Courtesy a private collection.

X P'-HAW-EEY-GHUN

The Buffalo Medicine Cult Dance

The wonder of Ah-tah, her escape and discovery,
The Buffalo Guardian Spirit, the sustaining force,
The men of Inner Power, medicine givers,
Offer the vision, the miracle of the mind.

—*Jim Asah*[1]

A KIOWA CEREMONY, PROBABLY EXISTING since 1822, is the *P'-haw-eey-ghun* or Buffalo Medicine Cult Dance. The dance could be performed only by medicine men. Because no authorized men of the Kiowa cult are alive today, the dance is no longer performed.[2]

The Buffalo Medicine was the strongest medicine for healing battle-wounded warriors that the Kiowas ever possessed. The following legend concerning the origin of the Buffalo Medicine was told in 1920 to Mrs. Susan Peters, a former Field Matron of the Office of Indian Affairs, by Chief Yellow Wolf, who was then old and blind. The story was translated by Spencer Asah, the late noted Kiowa artist.

Buffalo Medicine Man and Owl *by White Buffalo (Bobby Hill, 1976). The artist has depicted the awe and mystery of the Buffalo Spirit as the medicine man seeks Inner Power. The symbolic power of the moon and the owl heighten the drama of the scene.*
Courtesy a private collection.

The Legend of Old-buffalo-cow-woman

THE KIOWA MEDICINE WOMAN, was captured by the Pawnees during a battle at a Kiowa camp. Although she was carefully guarded by our enemies, she escaped one night and started across the plains to her own people. She traveled for four nights, hiding in the tall grass by day until she was far away from the Pawnee camp. She carried with her a large sharp knife with which she fought bears and wolves and other wild animals that crossed her path.

On the fifth day she traveled in the daytime, but she soon became so tired and hungry that she was ready to give up. She had found no water to drink for two or three days, and her moccasins were so worn and her feet so sore that she could barely walk. Suddenly she heard a roaring wind and saw a storm cloud rapidly approaching from the west.

Although she was a woman of the Plains, Ah-tah-zone-mah had feared storms all her life. She looked for shelter but could find none. She raised her hands to the Earth-maker, crying out for help and mercy. Suddenly she felt a great calmness come over her. She looked down and saw at her feet a dead, dried buffalo cow with skin stretched tightly over its ribs. Many times as a child she had played in such a buffalo hide, and she and other little girls of her tribe had hidden from storms in their "buffalo tipi."

Ah-tah or Pah-sho-hee (Old-buffalo-cow-woman),[3] as she is remembered by our people, crawled into her place of refuge sent by the Earth-maker. The storm swept over and around her. The rain came, and a little pool of water formed in a pocket at the edge of the buffalo hide. She had cool water to drink and to bathe her feverish hands, face, and head.

Almost immediately a second miracle occurred. In her hands appeared a buffalo bag filled with pounded buffalo meat, her favorite food. She ate some of the meat, felt strength returning to her body, and then fell asleep as darkness covered the Plains. During the night she dreamed that she was given a great power to be used for the good of her people and that she would return safely and would forever be a blessing to the Kiowas in sickness and in war.

At daylight Ah-tah awoke to find her little buffalo house shaking. She heard a fierce growling and knew that a bear was pawing at the buffalo skin. She rolled her sleeve fringes back, grasped the knife in her right hand, and crawled from the hide. The bear stood upright and growled as she drove the knife into its open mouth with all her renewed strength. The bear collapsed and soon lay dead at her feet.

When Ah-tah finally reached her people and told her

Ah-tah-zone-mah (Kiowa medicine woman) *by Richard Pemberton. "Ah-tah" reached her people after fleeing from the Pawnees and told her story. The Kiowas knew the Spirit Power had given sacred power to her in the medicine bundle— the Buffalo Medicine.*
Courtesy Richard Pemberton.

RICHARD W. PEMBERTON

story, they knew that the Earth-maker had given her a sacred power — and it was to be called the "Buffalo Medicine."

She later married a Kiowa and adopted two sons who became young braves. When they asked her permission to join a war party, she replied, "I am glad this request came from your own hearts. I have something I wish to give both of you as you face the danger and challenge of men on a war party. My gift especially helps those injured in battle." She then gave them the medicine.

After their return from the war party she taught them how to use the medicine and the songs. One of these boys, named Tone-zon-de-ah or Buffalo's Tail, was the great-grandfather of Linn Pauahty, who still preserves the original medicine bag. Tone-zon-de-ah and his brother later divided the medicine into several more parts, thereby making additional medicine bags. These bags are the Kiowa Buffalo Medicine bundles. The keepers of the medicine bags formed the Kiowa Buffalo Medicine Cult. At their deaths, their power was passed on to their sons or next of kin. As the years went by, however, not every man who received the Buffalo Medicine from his forebearer was accepted in the Buffalo Medicine Cult. We do not know why, but some men were not favored by the Earth-maker with the gift of *Inner Power.*[4]

IT IS UNEXPLAINABLE, BUT THOSE WHO became Kiowa medicine men did possess this inner power; they possessed something — a buffalo's tail, a bird's head — that was the source of their power. Only the medicine cult members knew the source of their individual inner power, but the tribe could see the results of that power.[5]

Those who sought inner power, as well as those medicine men who wished to strengthen theirs, were called medicine seekers. Once a year they chose isolated spots away from the camp, often on a bluff over-looking a stream called Medicine Creek in the Wichita Mountains. Seated crosslegged, the individual seeker meditated for four days and nights as he awaited a dream or vision which would either give or renew his source of inner strength. Though many sought this power of the Buffalo Medicine Cult, only a few received it.

The Buffalo Medicine men's practice of isolated meditation derived, at least in part, from the Kiowa recognition of a practice by the powerful buffalo bull. At a certain time each year the buffalo bull always cut himself from the herd and sought out a special spot — a tree, a grove, a thicket, a spot by the river — where he stood for days, seemingly in meditation without taking food or water. Even today the buffalo bulls may be seen doing this on the Washita Mountains Wildlife Refuge.

Those few medicine men blessed with the inner power were revered by the Kiowas, even though the power had its limits. Contrary to popular belief, the Buffalo Medicine Cult men did not administer to regular diseases such as colds, pneumonia, or smallpox. They administered only to wounds, cuts, abrasions, and diseases of the open flesh. Since battle wounds were their major responsibility, at least one medicine man always accompanied every sizable war party.[6]

In the case of sick children, the medicine man could administer his medicine, but he called upon the Spirit Power for help only after an open-flesh wound had been induced. Only then would his medicine work. The following account was given by one of the most outstanding women in Kiowa history, To-what-ta-mah or T'ow-hadle (Limping

Good Omen of the Medicine Man by White Buffalo (1969). Seated crosslegged, the medicine seeker would meditate for four days and nights while awaiting a vision or sign that would renew his source of Inner Power.
Courtesy Indian Arts and Crafts Board, the U.S. Department of the Interior.

Woman), known later as Laura Doanmoe or Laura Pedrick, who attended Carlisle Indian School and returned to work with her people for many years, even serving as their representative to the federal government in Washington, D.C. She gave the following story to Susan Peters in 1938.

T'ow-hadle's Medicine Scars

To-what-ta-mah or T'ow-hadle (Limping Woman), known in her later years as Laura Pedrick. When she was four or five years old she experienced the events at Elk Creek in the Kiowa legend about medicine power. The accompanying picture of her was taken when she attended Carlisle University, the first Kiowa woman ever to attend college. Photo by J. N. Chocet (ca. 1880).
Courtesy Smithsonian Institution.

Eagle Dancers by Stephen Mopope. The Eagle Dance was a friendship dance given to the Kiowas by the famous Taos Pueblo dancer, Tony Whitehead, decades ago. Courtesy Museum of the American Indian, Heye Foundation, New York, N.Y.

I N ABOUT 1868 WE WERE CAMPED close to the mountains on Elk Creek. I was sick and cried all night. I was in bed. Early before sunrise my father said to my mother, "Get her up!" I did not have any clothes on; she took me up, put a little red blanket on me, wrapped a sheet around me, and put me on her back.

My father led the way, and my mother followed with me on her back. I was crying, not knowing what they were going to do. They went south past the camps and stopped facing the east. Out there was a little pile of dried buffalo chips. I think now that my mother may have already arranged this as an altar. They squatted down and sat, looking toward the east until the sun started up. Then my mother laid me down on my back and held me, while she took a sharp awl and caught up the skin below my breast bone in the center of my stomach. My father cut it with a sharp knife; he held the flesh to the sun and prayed for the Spirit Power of the Sun to take that skin and leave me with them. He cut four pieces, holding them to the sun each of the four times and each time praying for my recovery. Then he laid them on the pile of buffalo chips as a sacrifice.

I was crying all the time. The cutting hurt me, and I was very sick—but soon I got well. My youngest sister, Mattie, has the same scars; she was made well from a hard spell of sickness in the same way.[7]

YEARS LATER, MRS. PETERS ADDED THE two following notes in

her folder to complete To-what-ta-mah's story. "To-what-ta-mah is now [in 1938] 74 years old, and the four scars of sacrifice are still rather deep scars above the waist line and above the center of the stomach." "When she died five years later [in 1943], they [the scars] were still there 'when the sun arose upon her life no more.' "[8]

The Buffalo Medicine Cult was recognized among the Kiowas at least until 1914. In that year Linn Pauahty, son of the medicine man Running Bird, witnessed what was possibly the last Buffalo Medicine Cult Dance held by the last six official medicine men of the tribe. Gathered to administer to the injured Richard Pauahty, brother of Linn, the medicine men were as follows: Humpo, or Crazy Bear; Humpey, or Brave Bear; Poolaw, Old Kiowa George; Conklin Hummingbird, a young man who had recently been accepted into the cult by the others; Paul Zotom, one of the former Fort Marion, Florida, prisoners; Pauahty, or Walking Buffalo, who took the name of Ta-ne-haddle, or Running Bird; and Fred Botone, who had received a medicine bag from his father, a recently deceased member of the Medicine Cult. Botone had not yet gone through the ceremony whereby he officially adopted the medicine bag as authorized by other members of the Cult. At this dance, therefore, Botone attended without official power.

According to Pauahty, the Buffalo Medicine Cult Dance usually began inside a special white Medicine Tipi, although it could be held outside. The medicine men never began the ritual until each had prepared for the dance by painting his upper body red, placing a buffalo robe around his waist, tying buffalo hair and horns on his head, and collecting the tip of a buffalo bull's tail.

Beginning the ceremony, usually in the early morning, each medicine man gently waved the tip of the buffalo tail back and forth in the direction of the patient. Each man held his own medicine bundle in the other hand and shook the bundle in rhythm with the drum beat. As the medicine men danced, their ritual depicted several buffaloes circling and hovering around a wounded one. Each medicine man in turn sang a medicine song. Two of these songs follow:

Medicine Song #1

I am the one standing on the trail of the Buffalo Power.
I am the one who gives the strength.
I am the one who gives relief to pain from wounds.[9]

Medicine Song #2

It is with my buffalo fur on my head,
It is with the tip of my buffalo tail,
That I move.
That is the way I work my medicine.[10]

His Spirit Joined Those in the Land of Spirts *by Robert Redbird. Medicine men could not always save a seriously wounded warrior. When a warrior was killed in battle, family members mourned him and in their mourning frequently cut off one or more of their own fingers in grief.*
Courtesy James and Helen McCorpin.

After the songs, the patient arose — if he or she could — and led the procession in single file out of the medicine tipi. The medicine men as a group then sang a song with no words, only vocables. Each medicine man, in turn, acted as a buffalo bull charging and goring the patient, thereby transfusing the healing power of the buffalo into the patient's body.

During his charge, each medicine man actually blew multi-colored paint from his mouth onto the body of the patient. The paint also contained healing power. Running Bird always used orange, red, and grey-white paints, but as with the other medicine men the ingredients and mixture remained his personal secret.[11]

Kiowas today are uncertain about the duration of the Buffalo Medicine Cult. The dance has not been held for at least half a century, although individual cult members practiced for many years after the last known dance. But when the medicine men died, replacements with inner power became increasingly difficult to find. The following account found in Susan Peters' papers reveals the attitude of one possible successor.

In 1926, when death claimed Jim Asah, Spencer Asah's father, he had been the owner of a medicine bag for many years and was famous for the miracles he had performed as a medicine man. When Asah knew his death was near, he called Spencer and gave him a small buffalo skin bag. Spencer was afraid of it, for all his life he had been taught never to touch it because it was sacred and should never be handled by anyone except his father.

"What must I do with it?" asked Spencer.

"Nothing. Just keep it, and it will show you what to do," said his father.

With that statement, the old medicine man did what all those with the inner power did who died naturally. He turned his face to the east and waited for death to envelop him. His spirit joined those in the land of spirits. And we no longer have the Buffalo Medicine Cult Dance.[12]

XI AWH-MAI-GOON-GAH

The Feather Dance (Kiowa Ghost Dance)

They said the spirit force was coming;
They said the buffaloes and the braves had arisen;
But as the moon fell westward across the sky,
That was our story in the stars.

—*Lee Satepetaw*[1]

Eagle and Buffalo Head *by Roland White-*
horse. The buffalo skull in the Kiowa
medicine lodge was painted red and
black; the black half symbolized success
in war, and the lighter red half symbol-
ized the successful attainment of old age.
The eagle atop the skull represented
bravery and leadership.
Courtesy Oklahoma Today *magazine.*

Kiowa Feather Dance Prophet and Buffalo
Skull *by Jack Hokeah (ca. 1930). In this*
dramatic presentation with artistic
license, Hokeah shows that Kiowa Feather
Dancers wore the upright Sacred Feather
on their heads as a symbol of member-
ship. The Yellow Cross symbolized the
Creator's power over the four corners of
the universe. The dance ceremony sought
the return of the buffalo.
Courtesy University of Oklahoma
Museum of Art.

AFTER THE BUFFALO DISAPPEARED AND the Kiowas could no longer hold the Sun Dance, many of the tribe turned to the *Awh-mai-goon-gah* or Feather Dance. Other Plains tribes had a similar dance which they and the white men popularly called the Ghost Dance. Another Kiowa name for the Feather Dance was *Manposo'ti-guan*, or the Dance-with-clasped-hands.[2]

A time of desperation spawned the Feather Dance. As white men became numerous on ranches and in towns and forts, the buffaloes disappeared and the roving life of Kiowas as hunters came to an end. The people were forced to abandon their hunting culture for a sedentary life on government reservations where they accepted rations from federal agencies. In despair, the tribe turned to rumors of returning buffaloes and spirits. Without the buffalo, the traditional way of Kiowa life, including the Sun Dance and all things related to the buffalo culture, rapidly collapsed.

Long ago, according to legend, the ancient Kiowa culture hero Saynday released the buffaloes from their original home in an underground cave and scattered them over the prairie for his people. But finally, after many generations, the Kiowas believed that the buffaloes had been forced back into their original hiding place by the white man so that the tribe could be subjugated more easily. The fact that the buffaloes had been exterminated was too incomprehensible for Kiowas to accept. They attempted, therefore, through prayer and sacred ceremonies, to release the buffaloes again.

In a vision in 1882 a young Kiowa received the mission to restore the buffaloes. Known as a medicine man, he took the name of Pa-tepte (Buffalo-bull-coming-out) and began his buffalo medicine in a new medicine tipi in front of which he placed a buffalo skin on a pole. After a year of unsuccessful medicine-making, he announced that somebody had broken his strict regulations and that the Kiowas must wait until 1888 before his medicine could begin again. Though he died in the meantime, his claims and prophecies were revived at the appointed time by Poingya (He-appeared).

In 1888 the Kiowa prophet Poingya declared he was Pa-tepte's successor and would restore the buffaloes. Claiming his predecessor's powers, he prophesied great changes which he saw in a vision. He predicted that a mighty whirlwind would soon blow away both the white man and all Indians following white ways. Following the whirlwind, he saw a devastating prairie fire raging for four days and consuming all remains of the white man and his ways which had escaped the whirlwind. On the newly-cleansed land Poingya promised to restore the buffaloes and the Kiowas to their traditional way of life. He commanded the tribe to follow their native habits, to use only ancient weapons, and to wear only native dress.

Most of the Kiowas excitedly followed Poingya to his headquarters on upper Elk Creek near Lone Wolf's camp. The prophet, disdaining any method not native, made a sacred fire using the traditional block-and-stick method. He gave the sacred flame to his followers but withheld it from disbelievers. Among those denied the fire were Stumbling Bear and Sun Boy and their bands, whom Poingya derided for their skepticism of him and for their adherence to the white man's counsel.

As the months passed, the promised whirlwind and fire did not come. During the summer the prophet's son died, and Poingya promised to bring him back from the spirit world when fall came. At the appointed time, however, the prophet's medicine failed him. Discouraged and disappointed, the people listened to Stumbling Bear and Sun Boy and became convinced that Poingya had deceived them. The old despondency descended upon the Kiowas again.[3]

In those days of despair, the western wind suddenly carried a promise. The western half of the sky became blue again as the Kiowas heard of a spirit army which would arise as the white man disappeared and as the tribe was restored to the new earth and hunting grounds. Like shadows in a dream, their departed friends in the spirit world and the buffaloes would move again as the earth trembled. This was the vision and promise of the Paiute messiah called Wovoka.*

News of Wovoka's vision spread through the Plains tribes. In conjunction with the vision, the Ghost Dance heralded the resurrection of the returning Indian spirit host who would retake the earth.

Tribal tradition says the dance associated with Wovoka's vision came from the north, and the Kiowas were first introduced to it at the great Ghost Dance held on the South Canadian River in September, 1890, in the presence of about three thousand Arapahos and Cheyennes, together with some Caddos, Wichitas, and others. Sitting Bull,** the Arapaho apostle of the Ghost Dance among the southern Plains tribes, guided the participants through this first ceremony.[4]

*He also was called Jack Wilson by
  white men.
**Not to be confused with a famous Sioux
  Chief of the same name.

Sun Boy (above) became disillusioned with the prophet Poingya, as did Stumbling Bear. Photo by Alexander Gardner, 1872.
Courtesy Fort Sill Museum.

Stumbling Bear was photographed at the time of his disillusionment in 1892 by James Mooney.
Courtesy Fort Sill Museum.

Apiatan (Wooden Lance). Pondering the news of Wovoka's vision of a new earth with returning braves and buffaloes, Apiatan visited the Paiute messiah and became disenchanted with him. Returning to the Kiowas, he convinced many to turn away from the "false prophet." Courtesy Amon Carter Museum of Western Art, Fort Worth, Texas.

Lone Wolf, a supporter of Apiatan. Courtesy Bureau of Indian Affairs and the National Archives.

One of the younger chiefs named Apiatan pondered over the religious possibilities of Wovoka's teachings. Having recently lost a beloved child, Apiatan decided to visit the Paiute messiah in hopes of reestablishing contact with his child. Supplied with money raised by the tribe, he and a companion traveled northward seeking Wovoka. The pilgrimage proved difficult and, although his companion soon returned, Apiatan persisted. By walking, riding trains, working and searching, he found Wovoka months later in Nevada lying on a crude bed with a blanket covering his face.

In their interview, the alleged messiah failed to show Apiatan his dead child. Neither did Wovoka reveal any supernatural powers or religious insight. Even the stigmata (crucifixion signs on the hands, side, and feet) were not on Wovoka's body. Totally disillusioned, Apiatan left for home.

The news of Apiatan's return preceded him, and upon his arrival the Kiowas assembled to hear his words. In attendance was Sitting Bull, the Arapaho apostle of Wovoka, who had returned in early February of 1891 to "give the feather" as a symbol of ordination to seven Kiowa religious leaders. In this highly charged meeting many had their hopes crushed by Apiatan's negative report. They sat in stunned silence as Sitting Bull was asked to speak.

Sitting Bull claimed that Apiatan was both wrong and in the pay of white men. Apiatan responded by accusing Sitting Bull of growing fat and rich on Kiowa gifts. He refused Sitting Bull's offer to return the gifts, saying that was not the Kiowa way; once given, a gift could not be returned.[5]

From this time onward the tribe was divided concerning the dance. Big Tree, Lone Wolf, and Komalty supported Apiatan in his disenchantment. But Little Robe, White Buffalo, Poor Buffalo, Tane-tone (Bird or Eagle Tail), and others followed the Feather Dance priest, Afraid-of-bears, in his attempt to preserve religious hope for the Kiowas.

Afraid-of-bears reinterpreted the dance for the Kiowas. As a child he had been expected to die during a serious illness, but a Kiowa believer in the "Dance-with-clasped-hands" attended him and he miraculously recovered. As a young man, he dreamed and in a vision saw the religious dance of hope which he called the Feather Dance.

Afraid-of-bears organized his religious beliefs and presented them to the Kiowas. His symbols were the Yellow Cross and the Cedar Tree. He taught that life for all continues into the spiritual world. Afraid-of-bears ordained ten Kiowa elders, not seven as did the Sioux, because he wished to preserve the numerology of the ten sacred medicine bundles of the Kiowas. These ordained elders entered trances, communed with their ancestors in the spirit world, and relayed their messages back to the tribe.

Afraid-of-bears then began his missionary movement among the

Kiowas. He offered membership openly to anyone who took the vows of the Invisible Church. He established branch churches, and each of the ten ordained elders headed a branch. The principal areas of worship were as follows:

(1) Redstone, west of Anadarko, headed by Tane-tone

(2) Alden, ten miles south of Latham (now Anadarko), headed by Skow-day (Old Man Kody)

(3) Sugar Creek, near Cooperton, headed by Amauty

(4) Hatchetville, or Apache, five miles northwest of present Apache, Oklahoma, headed by Taw-ho for the Kiowa-Apache band.[6]

The Kiowa conception of the God-Head became altered at this point. The Great Spirit now had a son called the God-Son, but never called Jesus. It was declared that the God-Son would come to earth and re-create the good life of the old days. The Kiowas, celebrating these beliefs of the Invisible Church for many years, held tribal Feather Dances as prescribed by Afraid-of-bears during mid-winter (December) and mid-summer (July), if circumstances permitted. Hundreds of participants camped at the appointed site for the worship and ritualism associated with the religious dance.[7]

For the participating Kiowas the meeting for the Feather Dance represented an Invisible Church, originally administered by a self-appointed priest and his elders. Membership in this native church was open to all ages and both sexes. Upon becoming a member, the participant received one of the thirteen feathers found in an eagle's tail. The feather, in effect the church membership card, was worn straight up or crossways in the scalp lock. Some original members claimed the feather should only be worn straight up.

The Kiowa Feather Dance priest followed a ritual which included prayers for meditation, devotion, praise, resurrection, and judgment day. The prayers, always to Dom-oye-alm-daw-k'hee as the Earth-Creator and Spirit Power, and to the son of the Spirit Power — never called Jesus — were as follows:[8]

Big Tree, a supporter of Apiatan. Courtesy Amon Carter Museum of Western Art, Fort Worth, Texas.

Tane-tone, a supporter of Afraid-of-bears. Courtesy Susan Peters estate and Helen McCorpin.

MEDITATION

O Dom-oye-alm-daw-k'hee, we turn to you alone,
To worship and pray to you.
We ask that God of the Spirit (Paye-tha-daw-kee)
May bring a message from above to all of us.

DEVOTION

We must turn to Dom-oye-alm-daw-k'hee in prayer,
He will make our hearts happy,
And satisfy us.

Komalty, a supporter of Apiatan.
Courtesy Fort Sill Museum.

The Crow was the symbolic bird of the
Kiowa Feather (Ghost) Dance. Redesign
by Ta-ne-shyahn.
Courtesy Oklahoma Today magazine.

PRAISE

When a new day appears,
Dom-oye-alm-daw-k'hee will bless you with happiness and joy;
Dom-oye-alm-daw-k'hee is going to see His children
  all over the world.

RESURRECTION

How wonderful it will be on that great day
When Dom-oye-alm-daw-k'hee will meet man in flesh;
  and all will see eternal life.

JUDGMENT DAY

I am the Son of the Spirit Power,
I will appear in the sky above,
And all the world will see me.
I will appear and come in the white clouds,
And all shall see me.
I will touch the earth with a sound like thunder.
  —Kiowa Feather Dance Song

The dance ritual followed the instructions originally given to the Kiowas by the apostle Sitting Bull. First the priest lighted a pipe and blew smoke heavenward as an offering to the sun; next, he repeated the gesture to the earth and then to the lodge fire. After smoking to the east, south, north, and west in succession, he solemnly offered a prayer for the welfare of the tribe, for help, and for the coming of the messiah. All stood while they prayed, extending their hands with palms down as they implored the messiah to come. Since the crow was the sacred bird of the Ghost Dance, the Crow Signal Song always ended the ceremonies.

The ten dance leaders, holding sacred feathers as the sign of leadership, prayed while sprinkling a sacred powder upon the dance ground. The sacred number for the dance was ten, and the ten leaders of the ceremony formed ten dance groups. Everyone held a sacred feather, which had been painted on a special day as revealed in a vision.

The body of each dancer was painted with a pattern seen in a vision. The multicolored designs included symbols for the sun, moon, stars, crosses, and crows, among others. The dancer's face was spotted blue with a red and yellow line in the center of his forehead.

To begin the dance the ten leaders entered the dance circle followed by their groups of dancers, all wearing blankets. The participants joined hands, intertwining their fingers and facing inward toward the cedar pole in the center while softly singing their first song. With the next song, their voices grew in volume as they moved about the circle in a clockwise fashion, east to west. The halting dance step was performed by slowly dragging one foot after the other, barely lifting either from the ground.

The Feather Dance songs were constantly repeated to produce a hypnotic effect. As the leaders waved their wands, emotions grew. A leader often waved his sacred feather before a single ecstatic dancer so that the dancer's eyes were forced to look directly into the sun, thereby enhancing the hypnotic effect. At this point the dancer sometimes rushed into the open clearing and ran in circles, or stood rigid with arms extended, or spun like a whirling top before falling into a trance, apparently unconscious. This part of the Feather Dance was called the frenzy, *guan a'dalk-i,* or "dance craziness."[9]

The Kiowas modified the Feather Dance when they held the dance apart from the other tribes. The Kiowa Proper introduced an assembly for worship and included a giant tipi in the ceremony.

Dance meetings were held in an extra large tipi entrusted to the priest, Afraid-of-bears, who became its keeper. The members assembled in a circle with a cedar tree (altar)—the symbol of everlasting greenery and eternal life—on the west side of the assembly floor. The priest occupied the center of the sanctuary on an elevated platform in back of the Yellow Cross. This cross symbolized the extensive power of the Creator over all four corners of the universe, clearly indicating that mankind falls under a divine power of salvation. The men sat in a circle in front of the cross; the women and children were behind the cross and to the rear.[10]

The women's buckskin dresses, free of ornaments and beadwork, had only a moon and stars insignia painted on the front of the blouse. The men had no special costume, but used hand bells and rattles made of the tips of deer hoofs tied together.

The priest, with the ten ordained elders to help him, sought a message from the spiritual world. Since the first meeting on the South Canadian River in 1890, trances and visions were associated with the Feather Dance. Trances usually occurred only after many hours or days of dancing. The Kiowas put their hearts into the dance, praying for a vision. Sometimes an authorized and consecrated elder went into a trance and communicated with a departed spirit. After all, the individual spirit never dies, but merely passes to the spirit world.[11]

The following are some songs of the Feather Dance adapted from the Arapahos and originally recorded as early as the 1890s.

EARTH CREATOR

The Earth Creator will descend,
The Earth Creator will descend.

The earth will tremble,
The earth will tremble.

Kiowa Feather Dance by Stephen Mopope. The artist depicted the Feather Dance women dancers at Redstone led by Tane-tone. Although originally opposing the dance, Komalty participated in the 1912 dance at Carnegie, as did Laura Pedrick. Courtesy Southern Plains Indian Museum, Lawton.

Honking Goose in Kiowa Feather Dance white buckskin dress with stars and moon design, near Carnegie in 1907. Photo by James Auchiah. Courtesy KHRS.

Kiowa Feather Dance Rattle. *This original Kiowa rattle, made with the tips of deer hoofs, was used in Feather Dance ceremonies held prior to 1916. Courtesy KHRS.*

Everybody will arise,
Everybody will arise.

Stretch out your hands,
Stretch out your hands.[12]

In this Feather Dance song the Kiowas voiced their basic beliefs or hopes. All the participants were implored to stretch out their hands toward the east and pray, thus hastening the coming of the Earth Creator.[13]

Dom-oye-alm-daw-k'hee, the Earth Creator in Kiowa belief, is the original source of all power in the universe. Only Dom-oye-alm-daw-k'hee the Spirit Power can create or halt creation, re-create or change the world, for he is the essence of wisdom and the divine source of worldly knowledge. In 1980 the well-known Kiowa religious leader, James Silverhorn, still implored the Earth Creator to aid his people.

THE EARTH CREATOR IS APPROACHING

The Earth Creator is approaching.
The Earth Creator is approaching.

He will give me a bird tail.
He will give me a bird tail.

He will give it to me in the top of
    the cottonwoods,
He will give it to me in the top of
    the cottonwoods.[14]

The "bird tail" referred to the feathers worn on the head of the Feather dancer. The Arapaho prophet Sitting Bull originally gave feathers to seven Kiowa dance leaders at the Ghost Dance in February, 1891. Afraid-of-bears continued the tradition, but he ordained ten Feather Dance leaders.

THE SPIRIT ARMY IS APPROACHING

The spirit army is approaching, tell them, (ba-d'al)
The spirit army is approaching, tell them.

The whole world is moving onward, tell them,
The whole world is moving onward, tell them.

See! Everyone is standing watching,
See! Everyone is standing watching.

Let us all pray,
Let us all pray.[15]

The Kiowa song proclaimed that the spirits of dead Kiowas were arising and coming like a great herd of animals. The ending *ba-d'al* indicated that the great arising and resurgence was only a hearsay report, not personally known to the singers.[16]

THE SPIRIT HOST IS ADVANCING

The spirit host is advancing, tell them (ba-d'al),
The spirit host is advancing, tell them.

They are coming with the buffalo, tell them,
They are coming with the buffalo, tell them.

They are coming with the (new) earth, tell them,
They are coming with the (new) earth, tell them.[17]

The above song reiterated the hope of liberation and restoration to the original conditions of the past. Again the *ba-d'al* (tell them) ending indicated the hearsay nature of the promised coming. The following song was self-explanatory.

BECAUSE I AM POOR

Heyé heyé heyé heyé Ahó hó!
Heyé heyé heyé heyé Ahó hó!

Because I am poor,
Because I am poor.

I pray for every living creature,
I pray for every living creature.

Aó ñyó! Aó ñyó![18]

In the Feather Dance song "He makes me dance with feathers," the singers suggested the return to the old Indian ways. The last line encouraged the wise old women, the grandmothers of the tribe, to "push hard" by throwing their energies into the dance and making strong medicine.

HE MAKES ME DANCE WITH FEATHERS

He makes me dance with feathers,
He makes me dance with feathers.

He calls the bow my father,
He calls the bow my father.

Grandmother, push hard,
Grandmother, push hard![19]

As the women danced at the great Ghost Dance on the Canadian River in 1890, one of the grandmothers "pushed hard" and went into a trance. In her vision the Spirit Force led her into the spirit world of her departed friends, where she joined them in the dance. Her vision supported the promise of the messiah. Her song reported her experience.

Kiowa Ghost (Feather) Dance depicted in the Dohasan Calendar, winter 1890-91, shows the return of a spirit warrior, symbolized by the black figure.

Poingya, also known as "The Messenger," was a Kiowa Feather Dance leader in the 1890's. He displays on a hide the vision he received in 1893 and relayed to Red Buffalo.
Courtesy Smithsonian Institution.

THE CREATOR SHOWS ME THE ROAD

The Creator shows me the road,
The Creator shows me the road.

I went to see my friends,
I went to see my friends.

I went to see the dances,
I went to see the dances.[20]

The Ghost Dance in the summer of 1893 at Walnut Creek was led by the Kiowa prophet Poingya, who assured Red Buffalo (known as Paw-guadal) that the latter's recently deceased son would be resurrected before the people's eyes. During the dance, Red Buffalo became "crazy" and composed the following song. The words indicated that he saw himself during the trance as a bird. He also claimed to have inherited the medicine power of his father, a tribal buffalo medicine cult man whose war cry was an imitation of a roaring buffalo bull. Against this explanation the assertion in the song that he bellowed like a buffalo becomes understandable.

No one questioned Red Buffalo's vision, but the prophet's promise was suspect because the boy was not resurrected.

I SCREAM BECAUSE I AM A BIRD

I scream because I am a bird,
I scream because I am a bird.

I bellow like the buffalo,
I bellow like the buffalo.

The boy will rise up,
The boy will rise up.[21]

A young man called Tongya-guadal or Red Tail often fell into trances and became known as a messenger to the spirit world. The statement in the following song that he "has been sent" indicated that the young man was recognized as a traveler between the living and the dead. "We hold fast to him" meant that the singers of the Ghost Dance song had faith in him.

NOW I UNDERSTAND! RED TAIL HAS BEEN SENT

Now I understand! Red Tail has been sent,
Now I understand! Red Tail has been sent.

We cry and hold fast to him,
We cry and hold fast to him.

He was made to live a long time,
He was made to live a long time.[22]

The Kiowas as a tribe disagreed over the Ghost Dance. Some claimed it was a cruel hoax, but others supported it enthusiastically. From 1890 through 1916 the Department of the Interior, Office of Indian Affairs, relentlessly tried to stamp out the "heathenish" dance, eventually withholding tribal rations and lease rentals from allotments until the Kiowas signed a statement forswearing the dance in 1916. Officially no Feather Dance has been held since then, for the Federal Government leased Ghoat-tsa-low's land where the Feather Dance assembly took place.[23]

Apiatan, appointed a chief by the Kiowas, also was rewarded in 1892 by the Department of the Interior for guiding his people away from the false messiah. He received a new house and a large silver recognition medal bearing the likeness of President Benjamin Harrison. In 1930, when Apiatan was seventy-three years old, the Commissioner of Indian Affairs authorized a $500 expenditure to paint and repair the home of the old chief and his wife. In 1980 the house still stood two miles southwest of Carnegie in Caddo County, Oklahoma.[24]

The Kiowa Feather Dance had a troubled and misunderstood history.

Buffalo Medicine (*Dohasan calendar, summer 1882*). *No Sun Dance was held this year because no buffalo could be found. The Kiowas believed the white men had placed the bison underground, from whence Saynday had brought them originally to the tribe, in a white attempt to subjugate the tribe. This summer a Kiowa medicine man had a vision foretelling the return of the buffalo and the Kiowa power.*

Kiowa Feather Dance, 1908, at Nelly Lancaster's house near Carnegie, Oklahoma. Courtesy Fort Sill Museum.

XII KAWY-DAWKHYAH DAWGYAH

Kiowa Christian Songs (The Jesus Road)

On days when my spirit is weary,
Daw-k'ee (God) makes me happy and I am grateful.

The kindness of Daw-k'yah (God) is good,
That is why I am happy.

— *Kiowa Christian Songs*[1]

WHEN THE DAYS OF THE SUN DANCE and the Feather Dance were no more, most Kiowas chose one of two roads — The Peyote Road or the Jesus Road. Some chose both roads at different times in their lives. The Kiowas have a legend explaining the origin of the Jesus Road.

The Legend of Aim-day-ko

IN THE DAYS SHORTLY AFTER WE Kiowas were placed on the Oklahoma reservation, a few Christian missionaries began work in the territory. The first woman missionary to the Kiowas was called Miss Reside by us. After she had been with us for some time, she enabled many Kiowas to know what it meant to be a Christian. In appreciation we gave her a new name, Aim-day-ko. Chief Big Tree explained the meaning of the name saying, "When we Kiowas see anyone on the wrong road we call out, 'Aim-day-ko!' ('Turn this way!'). And Miss Reside, our sister, came to us from a far land and found us all on the wrong road and in great danger. She stood in a new road, and she called to us and said, 'Turn this way,' and showed us the Jesus Road. So that was her new name, Aim-day-ko. God bless her always."[2]

INFLUENCED BY THE REVEREND J. J. METHVIN and by the priests at St. Patrick's Catholic Mission School, for example, many Kiowas who had sung to the Son of the Spirit Force during the Feather Dance now sang to the Son of God, Jesus. Using the traditional Kiowa word Daw-k'ee as God in translation, and Daw-k'yah-ee for the Son of God, the transition was easily made.[3]

The Kawy-dawkhyah Dawgyah, or Kiowa Christian Songs, included below are the work of Charles and Carrie Redbird (compilers), William Wolfe (singer), Louis Toyebo (translator), Moses Poolaw (adviser), and Lorna Gibson (transcriber).[4]

Mt. Scott Kiowa Methodist Church *near Lawton, Oklahoma; the site of early Christian activity for some Kiowas. Courtesy KHRS.*

EVERYONE, SEE GOD

Everyone, see God,
Everyone, see God,
   see Him in the spirit.
Son of God, Son of God,
   all look upon Him,
   see Him in the spirit.

YOU WHO ARE ON GOD'S ROAD

You who are on God's road,
   be happy.
On God's road it's good,
   it's good and it's true
   and it's good.
You who are on God's road,
   be happy.

LET'S GIVE GOD'S WORD FIRST PLACE

Let's give God's Word first place,
Let's give God's Word first place,
God's Word is truly far ahead of everything else.

Mural. St. Patrick's Mission School Opened, November 25, 1892 by Jack Hokeah (1929). *The artist blended the Kiowa Sun Dance symbolism in the two shields with the pictorial representation of the mission school. Courtesy Indian Arts and Crafts Board, the U.S. Department of the Interior.*

GOD, YOU HAVE HELPED US

God, You have helped us,
* and You have helped us.*
And we are rejoicing,
* in rejoicing we say thanks.*

THE SON OF GOD IS WITH YOU

The Son of God (Daw-k'yah-ee) is with you, be happy.
The Son of God is with you, He is with you,
* you be happy for He is with you.*
The Son of God is with you, be happy.

SON OF GOD, KEEP ON PRAYING TO HIM

Son of God, keep on praying to Him,
Son of God, keep on praying to Him.
Up there in the heavenly life He will open the door
* and you all will be happy.*
Deathless life He will give to you
* and you will be happy.*

HOW HAPPY I AM

How happy I am that God made a way for me to pass,
* my spirit is happy.*
God's Son the Spirit made a way for me to pass,
How happy I am that God made a way for me to pass,
* my spirit is happy,*
* my spirit is happy,*
* how happy I am*
* that my spirit is happy.*

I AM GLAD

* I am glad that God made my spirit happy,*
*   my spirit is happy.*
* It is God's Son that made my spirit happy,*
*   my spirit is happy.*
* I am glad that God made my spirit happy.*
*   One day my spirit was in distress, and*
* I am glad that God made my spirit happy.*

WE ARE ON OUR WAY

We are on our way to the Son of God's home,
We are on our way to the Son of God's home.
We are on our way to renew our spirit,
God, come near, come renew us.

Mural. Father Isadore Ricklin, Founder of
St. Patrick's Mission, in Council with
Chiefs by Jack Hokeah (1929). Catholic,
Baptist, and Methodist missionary work
in the days after the Sun Dance strongly
influenced many Kiowas, some of whom
chose the "Jesus Road."
Courtesy Indian Arts and Crafts Board,
the U.S. Department of the Interior.

A prominent Kiowa Christian song for those who chose the Jesus Road is one adapted from an ancient Kiowa one, although the words are not exactly traditional. It is heard at Easter time.

EASTER SONG

Jesus died on the cross for you
Let us all worship Him.
Because of His sacrifice, we enjoy "Heaven."
Today is a good day, because of what He did
    for us.

—*Ioleta Hunt McElhaney Tiger*[5]

XIII SE-NAY

The Peyote Road

O Cormorant, messenger bird, flying into the unknown
   to the heart of mystery and power,
And Father Peyote, eternal symbol, who never grows less,
   spread the rhythm of beauty, the Bow of Promise;
See, the Rainbow explodes, unleashing racial memories,
   and we find our meaning, our identity!

—Monroe Tsatoke[1]

FORCED TO ACCEDE TO MILITARY PROMISES, the Kiowas found life on the reservation similar to imprisonment. With neither agricultural customs nor a concept of private ownership of land in their cultural background, they were ill-prepared for government-sponsored farming as a way of life. Their cherished ways were forbidden, notable among them being the Sun Dance and the sustenance of the medicine lodge. Stripped of their traditional festivals, their religion became confused and their medicine was gone as a tribal force, even though the Buffalo Cult Medicine men and a few other individuals of great medicine still administered to them.

Denied the ceremony of the Feather (Ghost) Dance with its sustaining hope, illusory or not, the tribal members sought a spiritual anchor. Some turned to the teachings of the Christian missionaries and took the Jesus Road. But many chose Se-nay, the Peyote Road.[2]

Peyote was given to the people in a revelation. Throughout northern and central Mexico all tribes tell the same legend of peyote and the mescal bush.

The Revelation of the Root

Peyote Roots or Peyote Buttons. Four peyote ''buttons'' are eaten by each participant during the Peyote worship from sundown to sunrise. The hallucinogenic effect produced by the buttons enables the worshipper to experience a new reality through visions and reestablish his identity with the tribal culture.

LONG AGO A WOMAN AND HER people had left their village, wandering in search of food. The hunting men and root-gathering women soon outdistanced the woman, who has heavy with child. She was lost from her group when she gave birth. If the band had been in its home village, she would have had attention and care from other women. They would have sprinkled the ashes, cut the naval cord, and brought her warm unsalted corn gruel. But she was lost and alone. She took a stone knife from her waist pouch, cut the cord, and collapsed under a low leafy mescal bush. Buzzards overhead circled lower and lower over the woman.

Alone and stricken with terror, the helpless woman heard a voice speaking to her: "Eat the plant growing next to you. This is life and a blessing for you and your people."*

The woman turned her head, and the mescal bush which sheltered her pointed the way to the only other plant in sight. The plant, a small cactus without thorns, had a button-like tip or head divided into lobes. She extended her hand toward the plant, which miraculously grew outward to her fingers. She pulled up the plant by its roots and ate the lobed, button-like tip.

As if by magic, the woman instantly felt strength flow into her body. She sat up, looked at the rising sun, picked up her child and fed it at her resurging breasts. Gathering as many of the cactus plants as possible, she took her child and began walking again. The mescal spirit must have guided her, for by evening she found her people.

The woman showed the plants to her uncle, her mother's brother, a wise man among the people. When he heard her experience, he said, "This is truly a blessing which we must give to all the people."[3]

Peyote Meeting by C. Murdock is suggestive of the original woman and her uncle in the Peyote legend. Courtesy Indian Arts and Crafts Board, the U.S. Department of the Interior.

IN THIS MANNER THE PEOPLE RECEIVED PEYOTE, always associated with the mescal bush which first showed the way to peyote. Following the directions received from the woman, the people developed a ritual with its attendant symbols as they consumed the peyote button.[4]

Today Kiowa cult members customarily wear a necklace of mescal beans passing over their right shoulders and hanging on their left sides. The ceremonial regalia of the Kiowa Black Legs Society and of the Kiowa Gourd Dance Clan also includes mescal beans worn as necklaces

*Another version presents the woman and her ten-year-old daughter searching for food. They became exhausted, collapsed by a mescal bush, and heard the voice speaking to them.

Quanah Parker. *Comanche peyote leader*
in the early days, wearing his ceremonial
apparel:
(1) blanket of black and red trade cloth
(2) peyote fan for worship
(3) ceremonial sash, or necklace of mescal
*   beans, worn diagonally from right*
*   shoulder to left hip*
(4) otter or beaver hair braids on both
*   sides*
(5) beaded trim on ends of hair braids
(6) buckskin shirt
(7) neck choker and tie.
Photo by Lanney (1892). Courtesy U.S.
Signal Corps.

and as ornaments on buckskin shirts and leggings. Kiowa women sim-ilarly use the beans on the fringes of their dresses.[5]

How long ago the revelation of peyote came to the people remains uncertain, but Aztec priests were consuming the button before the Spaniards arrived in 1519. Peyote is eaten, never smoked, for it will not burn. The small disc-shaped tip is famous for its vision-producing powers.[6]

Some Kiowas say the Apaches gave them the peyote about 1880, but tribal members have known of peyote and the cult since the days of Quanah Parker, their Comanche ally, who used peyote in ceremonies around 1873.[7] Trained by a Mexican medicine woman, Quanah passed the peyote ritual to many Kiowas, including Tone-a-skawt* (Snapping Turtle), who was reputedly invested with an evil spirit but who never-theless became a powerful and feared peyote leader.[8]

Before Quanah Parker's death in 1911, additional support for the Kiowa practice of peyotism came from James Mooney, an ethnologist with the Smithsonian Institution who spent the years from 1891 through 1918 working closely with the Kiowas. In 1918 in a fiery speech at Darlington, Oklahoma, he urged Peyote Cult members to charter their "Native American Church." They did so, and the Peyote Cult was thereby institutionalized.[9] Some Kiowas have actively practiced peyo-tism since then. During the 1930's and 1940's John Collier, the Commis-sioner of Indian Affairs, supported cultural freedom and peyote usage by the Native American population.[10]

The Peyote Road is a highly personal one, for each member is on a quest for his own submerged identity; each seeks to establish contact with his individual guardian spirit. One Friday evening during a recent Kiowa peyote ceremony, a participant told the assemblage of his encounter with a Navaho poetess, Little Turtle, who had verbalized his own haunting thoughts. He relayed her poetic ideas as he remembered them.

EYES, SPIRIT, AND NAME

What is the look the eyes give
That reveal the spirit of man?
Some names give the inner self,
Kiowa names like Satanta (White Bear)
*   and Mahee-tane (Woman Heart);*
Names that reveal the true spirit
Which lie behind those eyes.
Tell me again the name you call out,
The name that is the spirit of you, the man.[11]

*Sometimes referred to as Tonágat in
white men's books.

The participant then said no more, for everyone understood his need for identity as he slipped into introspection and contemplation.

Kiowas begin their quest by fasting twenty-four hours prior to the ceremony, thereby reducing the nauseous effect of the peyote. Besides denying themselves food, liquid, and salt, they often practice celibacy for as much as four days prior to the ceremony, thus enhancing the possibility of experiencing powerful flashing color visions derived from the hallucinogenic producing peyote.

Peyote ceremonies follow no strict form, although there are ceremonial rituals and symbols. Traditionally associated with the Peyote Road, in addition to the peyote button and the mescal bean necklace, are the smoking of tobacco, the fire and incense, the messenger bird, and the altar. Kiowa meetings are usually held in an all-white lodge, beginning at sundown on Friday or Saturday evening and ending at sunrise the next morning. The man in charge, the Peyote Priest, prepares a dirt mound which becomes the crescent-shaped altar representing the moon. A huge peyote button known as Father Peyote, perfect in shape and never eaten, rests in the center of the altar upon a bed of sage. A line drawn the length of the crescent represents the Peyote Road. A man known as the Fire Chief ritually lays wood for a fire before the altar.

The only woman with a ceremonial role is the Water Woman, responsible for having a bucket of water outside and to the right of the tipi entrance. Her water is available at midnight and at sunrise for the members who will be dry-mouthed from the effects of peyote. Frequently she is the person to be honored by the service that evening.[12]

The Peyote Priest calls the members by stepping outside the tipi and blowing four times on his eagle-bone whistle. He leads the members inside with a bois d'arc (Osage orange wood) cane as his symbol of authority. The first to follow him inside is the Drummer, known as the Second Chief Man. After placing Father Peyote on the altar, the Priest prepares the traditional cigarette of ground tobacco and willow bark rolled in a corn husk. He puffs on the cigarette and passes it to each celebrant who puffs four times. The Fire Man then lights the fire and prepares the cedar incense. The fire and incense symbolically purify the bodies and minds of the celebrants. All the preparations are now completed.

The Priest starts the ceremony with a prayer:

> Sayn-daw-kee, pity us and guard us through the night,
> We who are the eaters of this little herb.
> Let this meeting be successful,
> And may this honored one have blessings throughout life,
> May she become successful and old.[13]

Each member eats four peyote buttons throughout the evening, for peyote is the sacrament. Fresh peyote buttons are four or five inches in

Peyote Spirit Design *after Robert Redbird. This untitled design by the artist is another Kiowa statement that the Peyote Road is an individual and personal one; each participant and artist fashions his own interpretative designs. At the base is the peyote button, the spiraling smoke before the crescent moon-shaped altar, the cross suggesting a soul saved, three round symbols possibly suggesting the "Three Greats," and the Feather Dance fan.*
Redesign by Ta-ne-shyahn.

Edward Yeahquo, Peyote Singer, *in his ceremonial dress. He was one of the best Kiowa singers ever associated with peyotism, singing more than two hundred peyote songs from memory. His father was an original Peyote Priest in the early days. His attire is excellent peyote ceremonial dress.*
Courtesy KHRS.

diameter before they are dried and shrunk for the ceremony. As the members eat portions of the buttons, they soon feel the effect of the peyote. One of the participants prays:

> Let us see, is this real,
> This life I am living, is it real?
> You, Sayn-daw-kee, who dwells everywhere,
> Let us see, is this real, this life I am living?[14]

Under the mind-expanding effects of the peyote, the celebrants feel the presence of the symbolic bird of peyotism, the "Messenger Bird." For the Kiowas the bird traditionally depicted in their art is the *Anhinga anhinga* or cormorant, popularly known as the water turkey. But it could be·an eagle, a scissor-tailed flycatcher, or a hawk. The bird is the messenger bird whose design the worshippers envision in the smoke rising from the altar. The participants know the bird carries their prayers to the Spirit Power. The Kiowas prefer the cormorant because it is both strong and swift: strong enough to carry the heavy prayers of heartache and repentance, and swift enough to reach the outer limits of space where the mystery powers dwell.[15]

As the Kiowa artists depict the bird, the cross design on the cormorant's wing symbolizes a soul saved by the entreaties of the messenger bird.[16] Throughout the evening the Drummer's beats, the Road Man's Peyote Rattle, and the smoke designs spiraling upward in circles created by the Road Man waving his Peyote Fan serve as emotional stimulants.

The peyote members mentally see the messenger bird flying within the tipi, its outstretched wings symbolizing the flight into the unknown. The long neck, like the bird itself, is reaching outward. On its shoulders the artists paint symbols of the peyote plant which they have seen during hallucinogenic moments of the ceremony. Blue feathers used in paintings symbolically represent the bird as the authority for early morning when the closing, or morning, song is sung by the celebrants.[17]

As the members smoke and pray to the unknown, they establish and seal the relationship between themselves and the Spirit Powers. There are three "Greats," or Spirit Powers: *Dom-oye-alm-daw-k'hee,* the Earth Power, sometimes called Mother; *Paye-gha-daw-k'hee,* the Spirit Power and Sun Power; and *Sayn-daw-kee,* the In-Between-Power, or Messenger Power who is the unifying force between the Earth and the Spirit Power. The symbolic peyote bird, the cormorant or water turkey, symbolizes parts of this Messenger Power.[18]

As the ceremony continues, the Messenger Power waves back and forth through the flickering rays of light from the altar fire passing upward through the smoke to the tipi outlet at the top. New visible designs are created within the smoke. Anyone inspired at this moment may pray, and one entreaty heard at this juncture in the service was as follows:

> O Sayn-daw-kee (Messenger Power),
> Watch over me and save my spirit;
> The messenger bird listens to these prayers,
> The designs begin to come,
> The beauty of the day becomes apparent,
> The inspiration rises, often seen through a veil,
> Revealing itself as a geometric design or a song;
> The rhythm of beauty begins to spread.[19]

Peyote Visions by Robert Redbird (see frontispiece).

Prayers are not directed to Father Peyote, but they pass through Him as an intermediary to Sayn-daw-kee, the Messenger Spirit Power. Similarities to earlier Kiowa beliefs connected with the Tai-may and the Earth-maker are evident.[20] In 1891 James Mooney noted the coincidental resemblance of the rayed head of the peyote button and the rayed face of the Tai-may.[21]

During the service, members may give special prayers for a mother or a sick child, thanks for a family member who has recovered from illness, hope for a better future, or thanks in honor of a new moon.[22]

As the evening passes the member alternately eats the peyote, smokes the sacred cigarettes or pipe, sings and prays, and drops into euphoric contemplation. The door of beauty opens, and the member passes through. An inanimate plant may suddenly become alive, writhing in colorful greens, and speak to the beholding member of its forthcoming demise the next day. Supernatural power fills the lodge as twisting figures rise with the smoke of the fire; a song suddenly is heard, more melodic than any modern or contemporary one, and the member knows it as a song borne on the wind from the old days. His mind is now carried backward in time. Monroe Tsatoke, the Kiowa artist, saw the gorgeous Bow of Promise, the Rainbow, witnessing its explosion and perceiving conscious and unconscious racial memories extending backward through eons of time.[23] The Rainbow linked him with the past and enabled him to soar above the present. He sensed the delicate balance between existence and extinction, and intuitively knew that the Kiowa language and traditions must be preserved. For without the past expressed in the emotion-filled words of the Kiowas, all moments of laughter and tears, joys and tragedies were forever lost. And so he prayed to Sayn-daw-kee, the Peyote Powerful Spirit:

> O Sayn-daw-kee, mystery and power,
> The ancient medicine wheel encompassed
>   our original world;
> Powerful, from the Sun, it gave us Tah'-lee,
> Some say it is a Wheel of Dreams,

Messenger Bird Between the Earth and the Greats by Monroe Tsatoke. This was Tsatoke's final painting before his death which was left at Susan Peters' door by his widow.
Courtesy Scott Tonemah.

But others know it as a Wheel of Wonder.
See us through eternal life.[24]

As he finished praying, Tsatoke knew that the exhilarating visions of the great tribal past restored both his identity and his dignity. He visualized the days of his father, Hunting Horse, and the lives of two of the greatest war chiefs of the Kiowas, Satanta and Satank, whose blood flowed in his four children through his wife, their granddaughter, Edna. As he witnessed these images, the euphoric cloud removed him from the chasm of desperation. The peyote ceremonial symbols and authentic religious visions were subjects which Tsatoke, evoking memories for all Kiowas, painted and explained before his untimely death from tuberculosis at the age of thirty-three.[25]

At midnight the sacramental feasting and smoking temporarily cease. The Priest steps outside the tipi and blows on his whistle four times to call the Water Woman and her bucket inside. After receiving a prayer of blessing from the Priest, she walks counterclockwise to serve water, first to the Priest and then to the other participants. As each takes four

swallows of water, she receives another prayer of blessing and then departs until called at sunrise, when the ceremony is repeated.

After the midnight water ceremony the Fire Man adds dry cedar to the smouldering coals. Created by the Earth-maker, the pure and ever-green cedar represents eternal life. The Fire Man heaps the ashes in two mounds shaped like the cormorant's wings. At the base of the mounds some lines are made in the ashes to resemble feathers. A third mound at the base between the other two represents the bird's tail.

Gazing at the structure in the ashes, the members receive inspiration from the designs of the great bird. No two people see the design in the same way, and an infinite variety of new designs for arts and crafts are continually discovered. A tiny notch on the bird's wing tips, for example, has provided the inspiration for the beadwork design on a gourd used in the Kiowa Gourd Dance. Shadowy lines in the mounds created by the flickering yellow flames are reproduced as feather tassels on many Kiowa objects.

Excited by the design possibilities inspired by the ceremony, Tsatoke produced many designs as did his associate, Stephen Mopope. In gratitude for these inspirations, Tsatoke offered the following prayer to the Messenger Power:

> O Sayn-daw-kee, messenger power,
> Pity me and guide me on the right road of life.[26]

There are thousands of peyote prayers, and as many thousands of designs as there are nightly twirls of smoke. The celebrants pray to the great unknown mystery which can only be called Light. Again Tsatoke offered a prayer to the mystery:

> Have pity on my crude
> manner of praying.
> Help me by revealing
> the great Light.[27]

Another prayer goes as follows:

> O Sayn-daw-kee, Powerful Peyote Spirit,
> I do not know one little part of you,
> Not even one little cotton substance of you,
> But help me to understand.
> As each bead is part of your design,
> Help me to know your will,
> Your design for me.[28]

Shortly before sunrise, the Ohoma or Kiowa War Dance has been performed on rare occasions in the lodge, but only if the dancer held the ceremonial dance in the deepest of reverence. The emblem of the Ohoma Society is the peculiar bird-tail piece; and the head of the Ohoma order about 1910-1920 was known as the "Keeper of the Bird."[29] Besides serving as the messenger, the Water Bird or cormorant symbol-

Peyote Rattle. This old Kiowa peyote rattle was obtained by James Mooney during his days with the tribe. Courtesy Smithsonian Institution.

The Bow of Promise by Donna Jean
Tsatoke (1968). This peyote design of the
rainbow was made with seed beads.
Courtesy Oklahoma Indian Arts and
Crafts Cooperative, Anadarko.

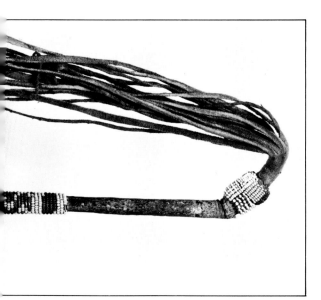

ically suggests peace and guidance. Its feathers are used in connection
with prayers because of its swiftness in flight to deliver the reverential
messages. The Water Bird, representing the In-Between-Power, was
Tsa-toke's last painting, left on Susan Peters' doorstep by his young
widow as his final gift, and entitled "Messenger Between the Earth and
the Greats."[30]

At sunrise the Road Man concludes the ceremony by calling in the
Water Woman with his whistle. A final "Morning Song" and a prayer
follow. Women then bring food to the celebrants and a joyous reunion
with family members occurs at breakfast. The participants have made
their non-militant accommodation to the greater society, recognizing
the military and political defeat of their people but engaging in the sub-
tler war of the mind to preserve Kiowa culture against the white man's
social and legal pressures to become assimilated. The Peyote Road is a
Kiowa effort to coexist and remain spiritually independent in a state
dominated by the values and beliefs of an alien culture. Peyotism is
devoted to keeping old ways alive. The ceremony is their moment.[31]

A Note on Peyote and the Native American Church

As indicated in the legend on the origin of peyote, the mescal bean
comes from a bush; the peyote button comes from a plant. But the two
have been confused in the Anglo-American mind for three reasons:
first, the legendary history of the mescal bush and peyote plant placed
them together; second, ecologically wherever the mescal bush grows,
the smaller peyote cactus plant is also found; third, an alkaloid derivative from the peyote cactus called mescaline is often confused with
mescal because of the similarity of names. Mescaline is deadly poisonous and never used by the Kiowas or other tribes. Sharp distinctions
should be made between peyote and mescal, and mescal and mescaline,
but seldom have state and federal governmental agencies or the federal
courts done so in the past.

On April 10, 1897, the Legislative Assembly of the Territory of Oklahoma outlawed the mescal bean, whose bush is noxious and poisonous;
the law was interpreted to apply to peyote also because of the cactus
plant's mescaline derivative. At the same time, U.S. Public Law No. 33
forbade the sale or transfer of any intoxicants to Indians living on allot-
ted or reservations lands, and peyote was defined as an intoxicant.

Native American opposition arose immediately, responding that peyote was a sedative, not an intoxicant. They pointed out that it was non-
addictive, although hallucinogenic. For the first half of the twentieth
century, the Native American Church went semi-underground. In 1969
a court decision in Dallas, Texas, said that only members of the Native
American Church could own, transport, and use peyote in its natural
state for religious purposes; for all others, it was forbidden.

XIV TIAN-PAYE (TIAH-PAH)

The Kiowa Gourd Dance

Spawned on the field of blood,
Colored by the Tdiepei-ai-gah, skunkberry red,
Taught by Red Wolf's vision, his dance,
The Whip, Rope, and Bugle proclaim us.

—James Auchiah[1]

KIOWA TRIBAL ELDERS SAY THAT AFTER the winter snows there will be a first thunder. The sound shakes the earth and awakens the plants, insects, and animals from their long winter's sleep. This first thunder signifies the coming of spring and tells the Kiowa Gourd Clan leaders that it is time to prepare for the summer ceremonials. The leaders make a pilgrimage and offer to the Creator a prayer of thanks for guiding the Kiowas through the year and a prayer of supplication for another safe and bountiful season. After the prayers are said, the members eagerly look forward to the Fourth of July, when once again they can enjoy life and fellowship with other Kiowa Gourd Clan members and witness the Gourd Dance.[2]

In this age of mobility, the gourd dance has spread across the nation. Many tribes have formed gourd clubs or clans, and the popularity of this dance can be observed at most Indian gatherings. Though each tribe has its own singers for the gourd songs, the Kiowas believe that the full measure of the dance's melodic beauty and historical significance can only be realized by experiencing and understanding the spiritual meaning of the original Kiowa version. The Kiowa Gourd Dance is culturally tied to a famous Kiowa legend. Without knowledge of the legend, one cannot fully understand the significance of the Gourd Dance.

The Red Wolf Legend

LONG AGO A KIOWA WARRIOR MOVED SILENTLY across the Plains, his eyes focused upon the distant foothills. Several days earlier he had been separated from his war party, and he had traveled without stopping in hopes of rejoining his people at their summer encampment. Confident that the Kiowas were camped beyond the rolling foothills, he forgot his hunger and thirst while thinking of his happy

Peyote Symbols: The Messenger Power by Kevin Tonips.
Courtesy Jon Christopher Boyd.

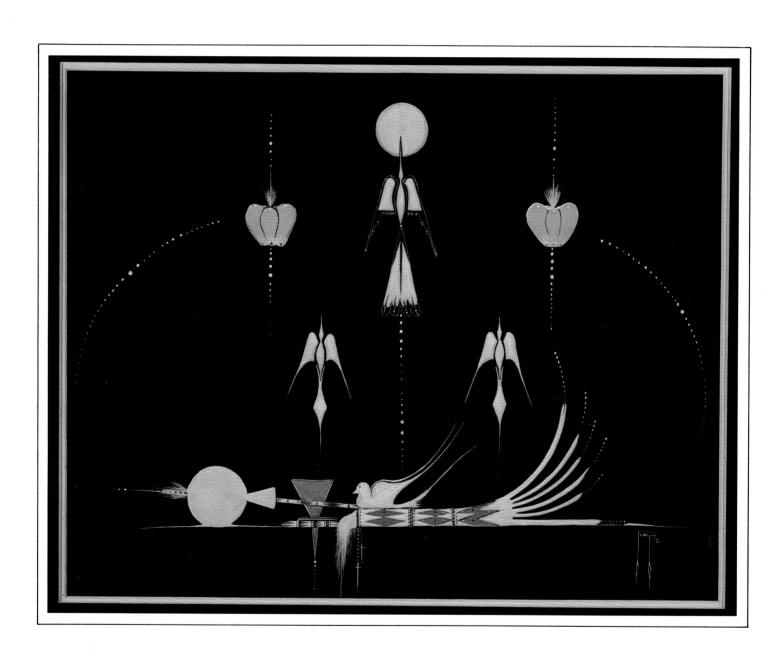

homecoming.

Suddenly, against the stillness of the summer afternoon, he heard a strong and clear voice singing a melodious strain. He knew he had never heard such a beautiful melody. The music stirred within him a haunting feeling that he was hearing something related to his past. He quickly moved toward the sound, as if he hoped to capture it before the prairie breeze scattered it.

The sound carried him to the top of a nearby knoll. He cautiously peered over the rim and saw a beautiful red wolf at the bottom of a grassy ravine. Red Wolf held in his right paw a gourd that he shook with a pulsating movement. His body moved rhythmically up and down in tempo with the beautiful songs pouring from his long, lean throat.

Time stood still for the young warrior as the entire universe seemed to join him in his suspended state. Through the long night he remained immobile as he listened to song after song. When the first glimmerings of a new day approached, he felt as if his total being were filled with new sounds of music that threatened at any moment to rise up and explode from his body.

As the dawn introduced another day, Red Wolf looked up at the Kiowa warrior and said, "I have given you a new dance with many beautiful songs. This is a gift for you to take to your people. These songs and this dance will remain with the Kiowas for as long as they protect and cherish their Kiowa ways. Tell your people to be proud as they enter the dance arena; and remind the children to listen carefully, for this is how the music will live. Go your way now, and teach the Kiowas what I have given you."

The warrior resumed his journey and by mid-day reached the Kiowa encampment. After he had eaten and drunk his fill, he related to the people his experi-

Eagle-tail Dancer *after a design by Stephen Mopope.*
Courtesy KHRS.

Kiowa Gourd Dancers *by Dennis Belindo (1968).*
Courtesy Indian Arts and Craft Board, the U.S. Department of the Interior.

ence with Red Wolf. The people listened, and they accepted the Gourd Dance with its beautiful melodies. To show their appreciation to Red Wolf, the Kiowas end each song with a wolf cry and a special shake of their gourds. And this is why we have the Gourd Dance[3]

THE KIOWA GOURD DANCE HAS TRADITIONALLY been preserved by the Kiowa Gourd Society. The society was originally a Kiowa fraternity of warriors and chiefs, dating from 1838.

After one of the greatest battles in their history, the Kiowas offered their gratitude for survival. Their victory at the juncture where Wolf Creek joins the Canadian River against the combined Cheyenne and Arapaho forces called for a dance celebration. Following the dance, the Gourd Dance fraternity was formed. The history of the society and its traditions have been handed down from one generation to the next, and they became culturally vital in the last decade of the nineteenth century.[4]

In the summer of 1890 the Kiowas were gathered at the Phee-hote, the "Peninsula in the River," east of the present site of Carnegie, Oklahoma. The tribe was preparing for the annual Sun Dance. During the third "Getting Ready Day" they had erected the sacred Center Pole when a runner brought a message from Chief Stumbling Bear. He had not joined the people because he was in mourning over the death of a son.

The runner informed the tribe that Government Agent Charles E. Adams and some Fort Sill soldiers were coming to stop the Sun Dance ceremony. That was the last Kiowa attempt to hold an official Sun Dance, for federal intervention abolished the ceremony. But from 1890 until the late 1930's, summer dances were held even though there could be no official recognition by the Kiowa tribe. As a result, the federal government did not completely succeed in eliminating all Kiowa cultural elements.[5]

By 1938, however, the Gourd Society traditions had nearly vanished. The dance was no longer held and knowledge of it grew dim. The songs accompanying the dance were seldom heard.

Finally, in 1955 Fred Tsoodle of Mountain View, Oklahoma, called together some Kiowas who once had been acquainted with the dance and its songs. Within two years the Tian-paye, popularly known as the Tiah-pah Society, was formally reorganized on January 30, 1957. After a lapse of twenty years, the society again presented the Kiowa Gourd Dance in 1958. Today the Kiowa Gourd Dance has replaced the annual Sun Dance, and the celebration occurs around July 4, the approximate date of the original Sun Dance.[6]

Kiowa Skin Painting of Sun Dance and Peyote Worship. *This Kiowa painting of earlier times shows the evolution of Kiowa worship from the Sun Dance (left) to the Peyote worship (right) and presages the Gourd Dance (lower left).* Courtesy Smithsonian Institution.

The Gourd Society bears a Kiowa name, Tdiepeigah. One tradition declares that for four days during the great battle against the Cheyennes and Arapahos, the Kiowas fought on a battleground of skunkberry (*tdie-pei-ai-gah*) bushes. Not only were the skunkberries red and in full bloom, but the bushes themselves grew red with the blood of warriors from the three tribes. Because they survived, the Kiowas regarded the skunkberry bushes and berries as a powerful medicine symbol, and they called skunkberries "Feast Food." Today the red on the Gourd Dance Society blanket symbolizes the red skunkberry. When a Kiowa

refers to Tiah-pah fruit, he means skunkberry fruit.[7]

In addition to the Tdiepei-ai-gah, or red skunkberries, the Kiowa Gourd Society has chosen as its symbols the Whip, the Rope, and the Bugle. Some of the elders have recounted the following legendary episode of the Whip which may explain its symbolism.

O NE DAY A HERD OF BUFFALOES WAS sighted near a Kiowa camp, and the Gourd Society was notified. Since the Kiowa Gourd Society of old had the duty of policing and patrolling the Kiowa encampments, it was their duty to respond to the news of the approaching buffaloes.

The Legend of the Whip

The chief of the society gave orders to prepare for the kill. As they quickly but quietly assembled for the hunt, one young warrior, eager to prove himself, raced out alone and killed a buffalo. By his hasty action, the young hunter frightened away the rest of the herd. The chief and the society all agreed that his disobedience required some form of punishment. A whip recently captured from a white man was brought forth, and the young man was whipped for his misbehavior.[8]

TO THIS DAY THE WHIP-MAN RULES the Kiowa Gourd Society's dance arena. If the dance lacks animation, he pops his whip and all must dance. His whip assures him the respect of all Gourd Clan members.

Many years ago when the Gourd Society warriors still raided, the symbolism of the Rope had its origin in the following event:

S EVERAL KIOWA WARRIORS RETURNING from a raid in Texas were suddenly confronted by a band of Mexican cowboys. After a brief skirmish, the Kiowas retreated because they were greatly outnumbered. The Mexicans recognized Satank, one of

The Legend of the Riata

the great war chiefs of the Kiowas, and they eagerly sought to capture him. One of the cowboys actually roped Satank and was dragging him when Chief Lone Wolf galloped up and cut the leather riata with a knife. When the warriors returned to camp, the riata was still hanging on Satank. This riata, from that day forward, has been exhibited as a war trophy of the Kiowa Gourd Clan.[9]

THE LAST OF THE KIOWA GOURD CLAN symbols was acquired when some Kiowa Gourd members were raiding down south. They encountered some soldiers, and a skirmish began. When the fight ended, the Kiowas could explain the origin of the Bugle.

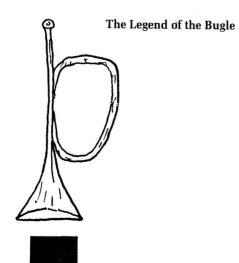

The Legend of the Bugle

ONE SUMMER AFTER THE SUN DANCE a Kiowa raiding party headed south. Eventually they engaged in battle a company of federal cavalrymen. The warrior chief Satanta noticed that the bugler blew different sounds which guided the troopers in their battle movements. He thought to himself, "If I could get that bugle, they would be confused!" With this idea in mind, he fought his way to the bugler, killed him, and captured the bugle. To mark his victory, Satanta blew on the horn and caused great confusion among the soldiers.

The bugle was brought to the Kiowa camp as a war trophy, and as time passed the Kiowas learned to imitate the soldiers' calls of "Charge" and "Retreat." The use of the bugle at strategic moments became a valuable tactic in Satanta's later battles.[10]

Satanta's Bugle (Keah-ko calendar, winter 1869-70). During a battle with troopers, Satanta captured and blew the bugle to confuse the enemy.

BECAUSE IT WAS ORIGINALLY COMPOSED ONLY of warriors, the Gourd Society has remained a Kiowa man's organization. Women have seldom been allowed to join.[11] Male captives who became cultural

Kiowas are the one exception to membership. The original membership of the Society was composed of the strong and able-bodied men who protected the Kiowas as hunters, fighters, and camp policemen. Selection for membership was made from warrior families, and the men chosen to leadership positions within the Society held their appointments for life, or until voluntary retirement. The departing member could then choose a descendant as his replacement.

Because of the hereditary system of appointment, certain positions were perpetually held within families. The most notable were those of the Drum Keeper and the Whip-man, who were in command of the dancers and the arena. Others were the four Headsmen, or directors, who had special dancing prerogatives. For instance, in the Opening Song, only the Headsmen could dance. Much of this tradition is still observed today. Members selected are still carefully screened by the Society.[12]

The Gourd Dance ceremony may not begin until the regular "Opening Song" is danced by the four Headsmen, as is their prerogative. The song, containing only vocables, usually is sung in the afternoon.

After the Opening Song is concluded, other dances follow with songs that have words. One of the popular Gourd Dance songs relates the last battle of Chief Big Meat, a powerful Kiowa medicine man who accompanied the Gourd Society warriors on their war parties.

During a battle in the south against the Mexican army, Chief Big Meat was shot three times in the abdomen. Big Meat and the party, recognizing that they were outnumbered, tried to escape. Big Meat eventually halted the warriors who were carrying him. He requested that they place him upright against a tree with a little food and water while they hurried on. He refused any additional aid or protection, for he did not wish to delay the warriors' flight because of his injury.

Then he sang his famous "Farewell Song" which the Gourd Dancers still repeat today:

> My warrior comrades [who have departed]
> Are calling me to the other side,
> Where all warriors go;
> I am now ready to join them.[13]

In former days special honors were given to the greatest Kiowa warriors of the Tiah-pah and other warrior societies. Originally the ten bravest of the Kiowa war chiefs within the Kiowa camp circle were chosen, and collectively they were called the Koitsenko, or "Real Dogs," possibly recalling earlier times when strong dogs pulled heavy loads and exhibited unpredictable behavior at times. Proof for an ancient origin of the Koitsenko is missing. The group was organized in 1838 and is mentioned in the Dohasan calendar in 1845. One theory holds that the society had its earlier origins in the extinct K'nataw (Spider), an

Tommascina Tsoodle Gachot and Taft Hainta at the Kiowa Gourd Dance Ceremonials, Carnegie, on July 3, 1961. Tommascina is one of only two female members of the society. Taft was the society leader.
Courtesy Fort Sill Museum.

"Keeper of the Arrow" Killed (Dohasan calendar, winter 1868-69). A Kiowa warrior who was the hereditary owner of a ceremonial lance was slain.

Death of Big Head (Keah-ko calendar, winter 1863-64). The owl's head is the death symbol; the gun indicates the weapon that killed the warrior.

ancient group that did things contrary to most men, things more daring and sometimes irrational.[14]

The Koitsenko were comprised of three grades, the first being that of leader, the Yay-pa-kow-gha or Black Rope man. Next were the three Yay-pa-guadal who wore red sashes, and the remaining six were called O'pai-yay-pa, for they wore blue sashes around their necks.[15] It was the Koitsenko, the greatest of the Kiowa warriors, who created the Death Song traditions and lived and died while anchored to the ground with the lance holding their sashes. Chief White Bear (Satanta) left his song:

> No matter where my enemies destroy me,
> Do not mourn for me,
> Because this is the end all great warriors face.[16]

Another Tia-pah song favorite has these words:

> This is the world where man is predestined
>   to die by sacrifice,
> Always in defense of others or himself;
> So today I, too, must be numbered
> Among that kind of brave man.[17]

Traditional Tiah-pah Society songs are few, especially when compared with the number belonging to other lodges and societies. Some modern songs with words have recently been introduced, but they have no historical significance. This society is conservative and ritualistic, and they have introduced little change over a long period of time.[18]

The Kiowa "Give-away" ceremony follows the Opening Song and the warrior songs. An integral part of the annual Kiowa Gourd Society celebration, the "Give-away" has always been a Kiowa tradition to show love for a family member, relative, or friend by giving away material things of value. In the old days when a successful warrior, chief, or medicine man acquired more than twenty ponies, he displayed his magnanimity by giving some to his less fortunate relatives and neighbors.

Today any Kiowa wishing to honor another individual will request the drummers to sing a special song for the chosen person, who will usually receive a give-away blanket or handmade costume. The honoree often dances before relatives and friends during the special song.[19]

The late afternoon brings a break in the ceremony, thus enabling everyone to have supper. In the evening, festivities resume with the required "Brush Dance."

Although the traditional evening events always open with the Brush Dance, the origin of the dance has been lost in the folk memory. Traditionally the Kiowa dancers line up in four lines outside the dance arena, one line behind each of the four Headsmen. Then the procession of adult men and women dances clockwise into the arena.

Today, the dancers hold in their hands something symbolizing a brush, usually a twig or small tree branch. The clue to the origin of the Brush Dance may be found in two nineteenth-century Kiowa skin paintings. The paintings show clearly that a Sun Dance is in preparation, and in each case a brush dance is depicted with the people being led by four Headsmen to clean the Sun Dance circle.[20]

Following the Brush Dance comes the main event—the Kiowa Gourd Dance. The celebrants perform the Kiowa Gourd Dance with pride and dignity. Once the Tiah-pah music starts, the seated men rhythmically shake their gourds in unison with the beat of the drum. When the tempo of the music changes, the dancers rise to their feet and flex their knees so that their bodies move in a graceful up and down motion which blends with the rattle of the gourds and the rhythmic beat of the drum. The Gourd Dancers move freely about the dancing area and take a few steps between each standing position as the rhythm changes within each song.[21]

Kiowa Brush Dance Origins: I. The Brush Dance apparently originated in conjunction with the ceremonies related to the cutting of the altar pole and the building of the Sun Dance medicine lodge. The brush ceremony is depicted in the two accompanying nineteenth-century Kiowa skin paintings. The brush is being brought to the medicine lodge site in this skin painting.
Courtesy Smithsonian Institution.

The costume of the Kiowa Gourd Clan has meaning for the Society members. Each dancer takes pride in being properly and traditionally attired. The Kiowa gourd dancer wears two strings of beads—one string of red mescal beans and one string of silver beads—draped over the left shoulder and crossing diagonally over the heart. The dancer carries a brightly decorated gourd in his right hand and a fan in his left hand. The traditional gourd dancer wears buckskin leggings, a red breech-clout, and a black shawl wrapped around his waist. The dancer also wears around his waist a fringed sash, which is usually trimmed with bead work. Kiowa moccasins have beaded designs along the side and silver cone-shaped jingles sewn on top and hanging to the outside of the moccasin; buckskin streamers are attached to the heels. If the gourd dancer has long hair, he braids it or wraps his hair with fur or brightly-colored yarn. One type of headdress is made of otterskin decorated with beaded medallions; the other is a roach made of porcupine quills worn

Kiowa Brush Dance Origins: II. *In this old skin painting the Kiowa artist lined up the four dance leaders in the foreground behind the Sun Dance priest.*
Courtesy Smithsonian Institution.

with one eagle feather attached to the top. A red and blue broadcloth blanket draped across the shoulders completes the gourd dancing costume.[22]

Kiowa women never start dancing before the men, and they never walk in front of the male dancers who are seated or dancing. To walk or dance in front of the men would be considered disrespectful. At times the women will intermingle with the dancers, when they are honoring one of their family members by presenting a gift to another dancer or to a spectator. But in keeping with Kiowa tradition, the women join the dance only after the men have begun.[23]

At a chosen point in the dance during a special battle song, a bugle is blown to sound the command "Charge." But the Gourd Dance is more than a Kiowa War Dance, for it is also a religious experience. As the evening wears on, the songs become torrential. The giant drum, accommodating eight to fifteen singers, throbs in the mind. The body responds to the Voice of Thunder; the drum beats are an invitation — even a command — to dance. The song has only vocables, but the Kiowas know its meaning, for it is an expression of the spirit.[24]

The drum beats and the singers' voices gather to the beat; the rattles shake, and the spirit of the people moves slowly toward the center of the universe in time. The Kiowas are again Saynday's people—the Principal People.

Buckskin Leggings *of a Kiowa warrior. Courtesy Smithsonian Institution.*

Big Meat's Death *(Dohasan calendar, winter 1874-75). The pictograph shows Chief Big Meat wounded and dying from soldiers' bullets during the last concerted outbreak of the southern Plains tribes against the white man.*

XV KIOWA DANCE, MUSIC AND SONG

1 Ceremonial Dance and Song

KIOWA CEREMONIAL DANCES AND THEIR attendant songs arose from the tribe as they experienced life and death, the excitement of war and the joys of peace. Each song had a purpose and was carefully formulated; each one was created to be studied and remembered. The Kiowas preserved historical tribal events and special individual moments through the song rituals.

Any Kiowa could create a song, but strict rules governed its use. The song belonged to the originator. The creator of the song might forbid its use by anyone else, or permit a selected person or family to use it, or give it to the tribe for all to sing.

Kiowas believed that unseen spirits were often stirred by the songs; offensive songs brought bad fortune while pleasing songs invoked the unseen spirits of nature and brought aid from the appropriate spirits. For this reason they had songs for everything in nature — the four winds, bubbling springs, painted clouds, the rainbow — because songs brought them in friendly harmony with all created things.[1] And they stood in good relation to the earth and its creatures.

Although Kiowas had individual songs, the great song-cycles of the ceremonial dances were sung in chorus. The Kiowas still regard ceremonial songs as a part of their living history, reflecting the glory days of the past. Some ceremonial songs once directed in chorus to the spirit powers were ritual songs in the Skaw-tow or Sun Dance, the Buffalo Medicine Cult Dance, and the Feather (Ghost) Dance.

In former times the war chief's invitation to go on the warpath came first in his individual "cry tipi" or Travel Song, calling the other participants to join him in chorus and perform the Buffalo (War) Dance with its songs. Wind (War Path) Songs, reflecting the loneliness felt by the warrior when away from his loved ones, were individual songs; the ritual songs in the traditional Warrior's Dance were sung in chorus. The Scalp Dance ritual sung by the women and the warriors' victory songs found in the Tiah-pah, Ohoma, and Black Legs ceremonial dances were and still are performed in chorus except for the individual warrior's coup performance. The individual Death Song and the group Mourning Song reflected moments of bravery and anguish.

Some critics of Indian music say that Kiowa songs are not music, but chants, and that the sounds are rendered on an imperfect scale. But the Kiowas point out that the white man's scale and musical tones have been derived primarily from his tuned string instruments. His voice follows the mechanics of a constructed scale called harmonic or chromatic. But the Kiowa has no stringed instruments, only the drum and rattle and flute. The only facsimile of a Kiowa fixed scale comes from the wooden whistle flute. Kiowas suggest their quavering verbal notes may have arisen originally from their attempt to imitate the flute; no one knows[2]

Roland Whitehorse caught the essence and purpose of Kiowa ceremonial music in his 1976 statement in Lawton, Oklahoma, prior to a Kiowa celebration:

> When we hear the Voice of Thunder over the Wichitas,
>   We know there is peace.
> When the Great Drum is quiet over the Wichitas,
>   We know we are at war.[3]

Whether interpreted literally for the past or figuratively for the present, Kiowas know the meaning. And when they hear the beat of the great drum (the Voice of Thunder), their imagination is carried afar amidst an upsurge of inner emotional feeling. For a moment their hearts cease to beat, their throats tighten, and then their hearts resume beating in unison with the drum. When the Headsman sings, all do his bidding as if under a spell.

Possibly the songs by the Kiowa Medicine Men of yesteryear produced the same hypnotic effect upon those who heard them. Today the old ceremonial songs still stir the listener, and the presence of the Earth Creator and the other Spirit Powers may be felt. Engulfed by the sounds of the drum and the vocables, the dancers sense the presence of the Great Mystery in whom they live, move, and have their being. Through their dances and songs the Kiowas drink of this feeling of mystery, this sense of unseen forces[4] And the Kiowas stand in good relation to the spirit powers.

The Ohoma Drum Design (facsimile) by Ta-ne-shyahn. The original Kiowa Ohoma drum contains the design of an eagle, the all-powerful bird from whence comes the Voice of Thunder, holding the thunderbolt in its talons; the edge of the drum is encircled with the continuous thunderbolt design. White Buffalo's grandson is the keeper of the drum today in New Mexico. Four legs of cedar, with a warrior's head and feather carved at the top of each leg, support the drum.

2 Non-ceremonial Dance and Song

KIOWA SONGS AND DANCES EXIST which are not associated with the tribe's traditional ceremonial dance rituals, sacred songs, and religious prayers. These non-ceremonial songs and dances have no historical significance for the tribe, but are social and recreational. The Shield Dance, for instance, is a friendship dance given by the Taos Pueblos to the Kiowas. The Eagle Dance of the Kiowas pays homage to the wild freedom and soaring spirit of the golden eagle, the tribal symbol of bravery and leadership. The Apache Fire Dance and the Caddo Turkey Dance are merely spectator dances enjoyed and painted by the Kiowas,

Turkey Dance by Stephen Mopope. Unlike friendship dances received from the Pueblos, the Turkey Dance is not danced by the Kiowas; it remains the property of the Caddos and is a spectator dance which the Kiowas enjoy and record in painting.
Courtesy University of Oklahoma Museum of Art.

but not performed by them. Innumerable courting dances and songs have arisen, including the popular Round Dance songs and the famous "49" songs[5]

The Shield Dance

THE SHIELD DANCE IS A PUEBLO DANCE given as a token of friendship to the Kiowas during the 1930s. As with all gifts, once given and accepted, the dance became a part of the Kiowa culture[6]

The dance depicts a sham fight between two warriors who battle each other with lances or tomahawks. The pattern of the dance is always the same, with the dancers moving on tiptoes with bent knees in time to the music of a drum. They move in a circle, gesturing and feinting with their weapons until one warrior overcomes the other with his skill and performs the ceremonial "kill."

Costumes of the warriors are especially colorful. The dancers wear elaborate ceremonial feather headdresses, short beaded and fringed buckskin breechclouts, beaded shoulder sashes, decorative wrist and ankle bands, and ceremonial bells hanging from their waists which keep time with the music as they move. Specially decorated shields carry each warrior's own medicine designs.

The Shield Dance performed today has no ceremonial significance; it is a dance presented for entertainment, especially enjoyed by non-Indian audiences and highly celebrated by Kiowa painters[7]

The Apache Fire Dance

ALTHOUGH NOT AN OFFICIAL DANCE OF the Kiowas, the Apache Fire Dance has found a place in Kiowa culture as a spectator dance. Kiowas appreciate the artistry of the dance, which may be performed today by only one particular family group of Apache dancers.

The Kiowas find the legend behind the Fire Dance unusually appealing.

The Miracle of the Fire Dancer

Apache Fire Dance by Al Momaday (ca. 1958). A popular subject for Kiowa artists such as Monroe Tsatoke, White Buffalo (Bobby Hill), and Stephen Mopope.
Courtesy Museum of the American Indian, Heye Foundation, New York, N.Y.

TWO YOUNG BOYS, ONE BLIND and the other crippled, were left behind when an Apache campsite was moved. With the blind boy carrying the crippled boy, the two wandered for many days, suffering from starvation.

As the boys rested on a particularly sweltering day, a supernatural creature appeared before them. They were frightened, but the spirit told them not to be afraid and gave them meat to eat. They built a fire and cooked the meat, and the supernatural being sang and danced. He cautioned the boys to observe everything carefully so that when they returned to their people they could describe the dance and sing the song for their tribe.

The supernatural creature danced and sang, and suddenly the blind boy could see and the crippled boy could walk. The boys returned to their tribe and told of the dance and the miracles. And to this day the supernatural being's dance is preserved as the Apache Fire Dance.[8]

MANY KIOWA ARTISTS HAVE GLORIFIED the Apache Fire Dance in their paintings, especially Stephen Mopope and Monroe Tsatoke. More recently White Buffalo (Bobby Hill) and Al Momaday have honored it in their works.

Courting Dances and Songs

AT CAMP MEETINGS TODAY DURING the evening young people build a small fire in the center of the dance ring. Forming a long line, the boys and girls circle around the fire and sing to the beat of an original Creek religious dance which is now the Courting Dance of all Plains tribes.

Later in the evening after the formal ceremony is completed, the young Kiowas perform the famous "49" Courting Dance. They circle arm-in-arm around the drummers at the small drum, singing:

GIVE ME FIVE MINUTES MORE

Give me five minutes more,
Only five minutes more,
Let me stay, let me stay,
In your arms.[9]

Multitudes of "49" songs exist. The term "49" refers to the glory days around 1849, to the dream days of long ago. The so-called "'49er" songs have replaced the old tribal War Departure or Travel Songs in Kiowa culture. Some of the songs are serious, others humorous, and a few are naughty. Some are even coquettish:

AH, I NEVER, NEVER CAN FORGET

Ah, I never, never can forget
The playful word he spoke long ago.

Kiowa Fancy Dancers, 1928. This rare photograph shows the famous "Five Kiowa" artists in their dance regalia, together with their supporters. Seated left to right: Monroe Tsatoke, Jack Hokeah, and Susie Peters; standing left to right: Dr. Oscar Jacobson, an unidentified dancer, Spencer Asah, James Auchiah, and Stephen Mopope.
Courtesy Helen McCorpin.

This man who seeks to marry me,
He with his sore-backed ponies,
What is he to me![10]

During the same camp festival, the drummers will sing Round Dance songs for the tribe, but especially for the young courtiers. Like the "49" songs, they are social dance songs with no historical significance to the tribe. A favorite is the following one:

JUST ONE MORE KISS

Just one more kiss,
Until you come back.
Hold me tight in this
    beautiful moonlight.
Good-bye, sweetheart, good-bye![11]

Wedding Dance by Stephen Mopope. The wedding dance is not an official Kiowa historical dance, but a social dance recorded by Mopope.
Courtesy private collection.

3 Kiowa Music

THE MUSIC OF THE KIOWAS FOLLOWS a repetitive pattern. All of
the following songs are performed with a rhythmic 1-2 even beat, with
the last beat usually accented. The vocal music is sung in phrases with
a chorus that is repeated after each phrase or verse. Although Kiowa
music does not easily conform to the European tonal system, a chromatic scale has been used for transcription purposes since nothing else
suffices.[12]

Kiowa Tribal Sun Dance

Rainy Nights in Taos

Thunderbird War Song

Song of the Evening Star

Little Mountain Maid

Music by Linn Pauahty; transcription by Jon Christopher Boyd.

TODAY THE KIOWAS ARE OPENLY giving recognition to their traditions. In the 1950s the Kiowas revived two of the old warrior dancing societies—the Black Legs and the Kiowa Gourd Clan. By the late 1970s the Ohoma Society showed signs of new life. All three organizations have revived their traditional ceremonial dances with the ancient songs and rituals. The growing strength of the Native American Church with its freedom of individual expression also reinforces the resurging enthusiasm in past tribal glory.

Although the tribal members have reestablished their roots in nineteenth-century traditions, they have not ignored the present. At ceremonial dance meetings they participate freely in non-ceremonial modern dances and songs of a recreational nature. The popular Round or Circle dances, the Oklahoma Two Step, the Courting and "49" social dance songs are becoming a part of the modern Kiowa way of life. As revealed through dance and song, Kiowa culture is healthily growing in the present while tenaciously preserving the glory of the past.

We Kiowa are old, but we dance.
    Ageless. Our dance is spirited.
Today's twisting path is temporary;
    the path will be gone tomorrow,
    but the folk memory remains.
Our forefathers' deeds touch us,
    shape us, like strokes of a painting.
    In endless procession, their deeds mark us.
The elders speak knowingly of forever.

—James Auchiah

KIOWA TRIBE
OF OKLAHOMA

Kiowa Tribal Logo by Roland Whitehorse.
This official logo of the Kiowa tribe shows
a Kiowa warrior of the Plains. The
symbolism includes ten eagle feathers,
which represent the ten Kiowa medicine
bundles deriving power from the half-boy,
Tah'-lee. The lightning bolt on the front
left leg of the horse suggests the Voice of
Thunder heard each spring and is
represented on the Great Drum of the
Ohoma Society as being held in the
eagle's talons. The blood red hand print
is part of the Koitsenko warrior tradition.
The shield depicts the sacred Rainy
Mountain in Oklahoma, the ancient
Kiowa burial ground at the end of the
great tribal journey. The recurring circular
patterns represent either the sun or the
moon, both important in the Kiowa
ceremonial dance rituals of the Skaw-tow
(Sun Dance), the Feather (Ghost) Dance,
and the Peyote (Native American Church)
service.
Courtesy Roland Whitehorse.

Footnotes

The Kiowa Historical and Research Society (KHRS) references are to specific tape numbers or folder interview topics. Principal KHRS suppliers of information for the *Introduction* were James Auchiah (grandson of Chief Satanta) on early Kiowa history and warrior dancing societies; Linn Pauahty (son of Chief Running Bird) on Kiowa history, medicine men, and ceremonial dances and songs; James Twohatchett on Kiowa tipis; Kiowa story-teller David Apekaume on Chief Sitting Bear and the Koitsenko; Lee Satepetaw (grandson of Chief Satepetaw and grandnephew of Big Tree) on warrior customs; Charlie and Carrie Redbird, Louis Toyebo, and Parker McKenzie of the Kiowa study group on the Kiowa language; and Robert Onco's papers on Saynday stories. Other oral historians for this and other chapters are included in the footnotes and are listed in the bibliography.

The Susan Peters Collection (SPC) references are to specific folders. The collection is an accumulation of personal interviews, Kiowa commentaries, memoirs and death-bed accounts of prominent Kiowas from 1918 to 1963 by the Kiowa Field Matron, Susan Peters. In the Introduction, the SPC provided information from the following sources: T'ebodel, the tribal story-teller, who was over one hundred years of age in 1919; Chief Yellow Wolf's dying account in 1920 of war path days; Chief Big Tree's accounts of 1922 and 1923 about his Kiowa calendar; Jim Asah's description in 1924 of the Kiowa Buffalo Medicine Cult; the portrayal of Kiowa camp life in the 1860s by Laura Pedrick (daughter of Chief Red Otter) in 1929; and Charley Buffalo's last account in 1943 of the Koitsenko and the warrior dancing societies. Additional narrations by others in this and other chapters are listed in the footnotes and bibliography.

Chapter I

1. KHRS James Auchiah folder, interview of 8-14-74.
2. KHRS tape 41, Linn Pauahty (7-14-75).
3. Momaday (1976), p. 27.
4. KHRS tape 53, society report (7-17-75).
5. Highwater (1976), p. 2.
6. Ibid., pp. 177ff.
7. National Geographic Society (1974), p. 14.
8. SPC Kiowa Lore folder 3, T'ebodel account (1919); KHRS Kiowa Language folder, Pauahty interview (1976).
9. KHRS tape 1, Auchiah's comments of Kiowa sensitivity to living creatures; also Momaday (1976), p. 27.

10. KHRS tape 21, L. Pauahty (11-15-78).

11. SPC Kiowa Lore folder 8, Jim Asah account (1924).

12. KHRS Sun Dance folder, George Tahbone interview (11-24-75).

13. Pauahty variation of Momaday (1976), p. 27.

14. SPC Kiowa Lore folder 4, Big Tree's statement (1923).

15. KHRS tape 42, Duke Tsoodle interview (8-14-74).

16. SPC Kiowa Lore 3, T'ebodel (1919); KHRS Sun Dance folder, Pauahty (1976).

17. KHRS tape 21, L. Pauahty account (11-15-78); interview (2-14-81).

18. Ibid.

19. Ibid.

20. SPC Kiowa Lore 2, Laura Pedrick account (1929).

21. KHRS Ceremonial Dance folder 1, Guy Quoetone account (10-2-75).

22. KHRS Sun Dance folder, Linn Pauahty statement (10-2-75).

23. Ibid.

24. Eddy (1974), 1035.

25. KHRS Sun Dance folder, Jacob Ahtone declaration (10-2-75).

26. *Oklahoma Today* (Summer, 1975), 26-27; statements endorsed by KHRS Ceremonial Dance folder 3, society consensus (4-3-76).

27. KHRS Ceremonial Dance folder 3, L. Pauahty interview (2-14-81).

28. Ewers (1978), p. 16; Little Bluff's "Battle Pictures" tipi.

29. SPC Kiowa Lore 8 folder, Laura Pedrick's discussion of Red Otter's "Porcupine Tipi."

30. SPC Kiowa Lore 1, James Auchiah account (1929).

31. KHRS Ceremonial Dance folder 1, L. Pauahty interview (4-3-76).

32. KHRS tape 101, Gomda Dawgyah or Wind Songs by Sallie Hokeah Bointy.

33. KHRS Ceremonial Dance folder 4, "Rabbit Dance" songs and society report (4-3-76).

34. KHRS tape 101, Wind Song by Sallie Hokeah Bointy.

35. Ibid.

36. Ibid., society consensus (4-3-76).

37. KHRS Ceremonial Dance folder 1, L. Pauahty (4-3-76).

38. KHRS tape 45, David Apekaume interview (5-10-75).

39. SPC Yellow Wolf folder, Yellow Wolf's account translated by Spencer Asah (1920).

40. SPC Kiowa Lore folder 8, medicine men traditions by Susie Peters.

41. KHRS Ceremonial Dance folder 1, L. Pauahty (4-3-76).

42. SPC Charley Buffalo folder (1943).

43. KHRS Ceremonial Dance folder 1, account by L. Pauahty (11-24-80), the son of Ta-ne-haddle; other versions differ slightly in Dixon (1914), p. 48, and in Francis E. Leupp, *In Red Man's Land* (New York, 1914), p. 87.

44. KHRS Ceremonial Dance folder 2, society consensus report

(11-19-75).

45. National Geographic Society (1974), p. 350.
46. KHRS Ceremonial Dance folder 2, society consensus (11-19-75).
47. Mooney (1896), 1081-87.
48. KHRS Ceremonial Dance folder 2, society consensus (11-19-75).
49. SPC Kiowa Peyote folder, Monroe Tsatoke account (1935).
50. Ibid., Mary Buffalo's account of a Peyote meeting, Sept. 24, 1923.
51. KHRS Sun Dance folder, George Tahbone's songs (1977).
52. Redbird (1962), p. 1; KHRS Kiowa Language folder, Charles Redbird account (8-4-76).

Chapter II

1. SPC Kiowa Lore folder 1, James Auchiah account (1929); also KHRS Kiowa History folder, James Auchiah account (8-5-74).
2. SPC Kiowa Artists folder, the 1936 interview with E-mah-ah (A-mai ah), the keeper of the Tai-may from 1894 until 1939.
3. Ibid.; also Laura Pedrick's recollections (1924).
4. Ibid.
5. Ibid.; also KHRS Sun Dance folder, song by L. Pauahty (7-13-75).
6. Ibid.; also KHRS Sun Dance folder, song by Linn Pauahty (10-22-80).

Chapter III

1. SPC Kickingbird folder (1920), account by son of Kickingbird I. The KHRS carefully reviewed the Sun Dance accounts of Battey (1876), Tatum (1899), Scott (1911), Mooney (1898), Spier (1921), and statements by Mishkin (1940), Nye (1942, 1962), Marriott (1945), Newcomb (1961), and Mayhall (1962) in their summary of the traditional ceremonial Sun Dance. On many points there was general or consensus agreement with the published accounts, but the Kiowas sharply disagree with those who claim (1) the presence of torture in the Kiowa ceremony or (2) the ritual control of the four dancing days by the Tai-may keeper instead of the Sun Dance Gourd keeper.
2. Carole Frame papers, the 1959 account by Robert Onco, son of Anko the calendar man; also KHRS Sun Dance folder, L. Pauahty interview (6-8-80).
3. Ibid.; also SPC Kiowa Lore folder 8, Laura Pedrick (1924).
4. SPC Kickingbird folder (1920).
5. KHRS Sun Dance folder, Jimmie Quoetone interview (11-24-75).
6. Ibid., Linn Pauahty interview (11-24-75).
7. SPC Kiowa Lore folder 8, Laura Pedrick (1924).

8. Ibid.; also KHRS Sun Dance folder, Jimmie Quoetone (11-24-75).

9. KHRS Sun Dance folder, L. Pauahty interview (11-15-78).

10. Ibid., L. Pauahty interview (10-22-80).

11. Ibid.

12. Ibid., L. Pauahty (6-8-80).

13. SPC Kiowa Lore folder 8, Laura Pedrick (1924).

14. SPC Kiowa Lore folder 1, James Auchiah (1929).

15. KHRS Sun Dance folder, Marjie Tahbone interview (11-25-75).

16. Ibid., George Tahbone interview (11-25-75).

17. KHRS tape 6, society consensus (10-22-80).

18. KHRS Ceremonial Dance folder 1, L. Pauahty interview (4-3-76) on the Kiowa War Dance (Buffalo Dance).

Chapter IV

1. KHRS Ceremonial Dance folder 1, Lee Satepetaw interview (4-2-76).

2. Ibid., Buffalo (War) Dance interview with L. Pauahty (4-3-76).

3. SPC Prayers and Poems folder with the account of Wolf-lying-down, by Laura Pedrick (1939).

4. SPC Kiowa Lore folder 8, Susan Peters and Laura Pedrick (1939).

5. KHRS Ceremonial Dance folder 4, society consensus (3-18-76).

6. Ibid., L. Pauahty (3-18-76).

7. Ceremonial booklet entitled *Kiowa Gourd Clan Ceremonials*, July 1-4, 1976, pp. 2-3.

Chapter V

1. Curtis (1968), p. 23; Eagle Tail's song slightly revised by L. Pauahty.

2. KHRS Ceremonial Dance folder 4 on "Wind Songs" by L. Pauahty (4-3-76).

3. KHRS tape 101 on "Wind Songs" by Sallie Hokeah Bointy.

4. Ibid., supplied by Soundchief recordings, courtesy L. Pauahty translation.

5. Ibid.; a similar rendition by Apiatan (Wooden Lance) was recorded by Curtis (1968), pp. 224, 231, in 1907.

6. KHRS Ceremonial Dance folder 4, L. Pauahty (7-3-76).

Chapter VI

1. SPC Prayers and Poems folder, account of Laura Pedrick (1932).

2. KHRS Ceremonial Dance folder 3 on the "Scalp Dance" by

L. Pauahty (4-3-76); also SPC Kiowa Lore folder 4 on George Mopope's 1919 account of his grandfather's (Gua-la-te's) Scalp Dance in 1854.

3. KHRS tapes 131 and 137 on Warrior's Dance Ceremonial, including Scalp Dance songs, by Nathan Doyebo, James Aunquoe, Ruth and Earnest Redbird; Soundchief collection of songs recorded by L. Pauahty.

4. KHRS Ceremonial Dance folder 3, Lee Satepetaw (4-2-76).

5. Ibid.

6. Ibid.

7. KHRS History folder, interview with L. Pauahty (2-8-81).

8. Ibid., song by L. Pauahty (11-24-80).

9. KHRS Ceremonial Dance folder 3, sung by L. Pauahty (4-3-76).

10. KHRS tape 301 by Leonard Cozad, J. Sakadota, Oscar and Laura Tahlo; also KHRS tape 45 on Death Songs by David Apekaume (5-10-75).

11. SPC Prayers and Songs folder, copy by Susie Peters; also L. Pauahty interview (11-24-80).

Chapter VII

1. KHRS Medicine folder, L. Pauahty interviews (12-18-80) and (2-8-81).

2. KHRS Ceremonial Dance folder 1, interviews with Lee Satepetaw, Jimmie Quoetone, and Linn Pauahty (4-3-76) on the Ohoma Dance.

3. Ibid., Pauahty interview (10-18-80).

4. Carole Frame papers, Robert Onco account (n.d.)

5. KHRS Ceremonial Dance folder 1, Pauahty narrative of the Ohoma Dance (4-3-76) and (10-18-80).

6. KHRS tapes 140 and 140A provide the Ohoma Dance Ceremonial dances and songs by Leonard Cozad, Gus Palmer, and Jasper Sankadota. Explanation of the sequence is provided in KHRS Ceremonial Dance folder 1, interviews with Linn Pauahty (4-3-76) and (10-18-80).

7. KHRS Ceremonial Dance folder 1, Pauahty interview (10-18-80).

8. Gamble (1951) distinguishes between the ceremonial and nonceremonial "Give-away" patterns; his M.S. thesis (1952), pp. 17-22, on "Kiowa Dance Gatherings" gives additional details.

9. KHRS tape 140A contains the "Closing Song" by Kiowa tribal singers.

Chapter VIII

1. SPC Kiowa Lore 8; Laura Pedrick (1925) quotes Ha-Goon (Haun-

Gooah) or Silverhorn and recounts her experiences in the 1860s. She elaborates upon the words of Seattle, the Duwamish chief.

2. KHRS Ceremonial Dance folder 3, interview on the Black Legs Society with L. Pauahty (4-3-76).

3. Ibid. Fort Sill Museum, James Auchiah papers on the society's early history and leaders, entitled "Black Leggings Society" (1973).

4. Ibid. See also Gillett Griswold's handwritten account of the "Black Leggings Society of Kiowa Warriors," pp. 1-8, in the Fort Sill Museum archives.

5. KHRS Ceremonial Dance folder 3, L. Pauahty account (4-3-76).

6. SPC Kiowa Captives folder, the George Mopope account (1919) of Gool-ha-ee's 1854 expedition and the Red Cape, as given to Mopope by Big Tree and Ain-koy.

7. KHRS History folder, Ta-ne-haddle's 1914 words for the coup stick as relayed by Linn Pauahty (2-8-81).

8. KHRS tape 305, entitled "Black Legs Society" provides the dance songs by Leonard Cozad, Oscar and Laura Tahlo, and Jasper Sankadota, courtesy Soundchief records and Linn Pauahty. Also KHRS tape 45 for Sitting Bear's death chants by David Apekaume (5-10-75).

9. SPC Kiowa Lore folder 5, "Satank's Medicine Arrows."

10. KHRS Ceremonial Dance folder 4, "Big Meat's Song" by L. Pauahty (7-2-76) and (12-18-80).

11. SPC Kiowa Lore 5, Satanta's and Satank's death songs by Susie Peters.

12. KHRS Ceremonial Dance folder 4, "Poor Buffalo's Song" by Pauahty (12-18-80).

Chapter IX

1. SPC Kiowa Lore folder 8, Laura Pedrick (1925).

2. KHRS tape 21, account of "Rabbit Old Man Legend" (11-15-78) by Gina Quoe-tone Pauahty, sister of Guy Quoetone.

3. KHRS History folder, James Auchiah's account of the "Rabbit Old Man Legend (1972).

4. KHRS Ceremonial Dance folder 4 gives society's consensus on the ages for Rabbits as 8 to 12; in the 1894 Mooney Notebook, Ms. 2531, Vol. 3, p. 7 (B.E.A., Washington, D.C.) the ages are listed as 10-15.

5. SPC Kiowa Lore folder 1, James Auchiah account (n.d.); also KHRS tape 21, Gina Quoe-tone Pauahty (11-15-78).

6. KHRS Sun Dance folder, George Tahbone interview (11-25-75) on the Rabbit Dance.

7. KHRS Ceremonial Dance folder 4, song by Linn Pauahty.

8. Ibid.
9. KHRS tape 21, Gina Quoe-tone Pauahty (11-15-78).

Chapter X

1. SPC Kiowa Lore folder 8, translation by Spencer Asah of his father's statements (1925).
2. KHRS Ceremonial Dance folder 1, Lee Satepetaw and Linn Pauahty account (4-2-76).
3. SPC Yellow Wolf folder, account by Chief Yellow Wolf as translated by Spencer Asah (1920).
4. KHRS tape 47 has another similar version of the Ah-tah-zone-mah (Ah-tah-skon-mah) story by David Apekaume (7-2-76).
5. Ibid.
6. KHRS Ceremonial Dance folder 1, account by Linn Pauahty, son of one of the last Buffalo Medicine Cult men (4-3-76).
7. SPC Kiowa Lore folder 8, account by Laura Pedrick (1938).
8. Ibid., with notes added to the Pedrick account by Susie Peters in 1939 and 1943.
9. KHRS Ceremonial Dance folder 1, remembrances by Linn Pauahty (4-3-76).
10. Ibid.
11. Ibid.
12. SPC Kiowa Lore folder 8, account by Susie Peters (1926).

Chapter XI

1. KHRS Ceremonial Dance folder 2, account of Lee Satepetaw (9-13-75). Also the complaints of Big Tree, Lone Wolf, Komalty, and Chaddlehaungky are voiced in their letter to Captain Frank Baldwin, dated 4-27-96, asking for better treatment and guidance. Courtesy Oklahoma Historical Society, Indian Archives.

   The KHRS examined in detail the "Ghost Dance" accounts by many authorities, including Mooney (1896), Nye (1937), Mayhall (1962), Brown (1970), Laubin (1977) and Highwater (1977), among others. The society insists that their name for their dance, the Feather Dance, indicates the unique, non-militant characteristics absent in the "Ghost Dance" of the northern Plains tribes.
2. Ibid.; also Mooney (1896, 1081-1087) reports this name reference. *The Anadarko Daily News* (8-11-57) describes the early Kiowa Feather (Ghost) Dance.
3. S. Vestal (1948) builds this thesis; also KHRS Ceremonial Dance folder 2, Yale Spottedbird (12-20-77).
4. KHRS Ceremonial Dance folder 2, Lee Satepetaw (4-2-76); also

society consensus of 11-19-75.

5. Ibid.

6. Ibid.; also SPC Kickingbird folder, Kickingbird statements (1920).

7. Carole Frame papers, Robert Onco's written statement (ca. 1959).

8. KHRS Ceremonial Dance folder 2, society's report (11-19-75).

9. KHRS tape 43, society's report with the qualification that the trance was a rarity usually experienced only under careful supervision of a Feather Dance priest.

10. KHRS Ceremonial Dance folder 2, Pauahty's accounts (4-3-76) and (11-18-80).

11. SPC Kiowa Lore folder 8, Laura Pedrick (1929).

12. KHRS tape 43, Linn Pauahty song (7-14-74).

13. Ibid.; source also in Mooney (1894).

14. Ibid.

15. KHRS Ceremonial Dance folder 2, Linn Pauahty interview (12-18-80), has only a slight variation from Mooney (1894). The KHRS says the word *ba-d'al*, not Mooney's *hédal*, is a more accurate rendition of their pronounced word which means "they say."

16. Ibid.

17. Ibid.

18. Ibid.

19. Ibid.; Mooney (1896) inaccurately said "arrows" instead of "feathers," which the Kiowas insist is the correct meaning in translation.

20. Ibid.; also Mooney (1896).

21. Ibid.

22. Ibid.

23. Letter of T. P. Morgan, B.I.A. Commissioner, Dept. of the Interior (1-2-92), orders the Kiowa Ghost Dance to be stopped. Copy courtesy the Oklahoma Historical Society. Also KHRS tape 21 (11-15-78) and Pauahty interview (12-18-80).

24. Letter of authorization of $500 from the B.I.A. collection of photographs includes a picture of Apiatan, his wife, and the renovated home in 1930; the KHRS reports the house still stands southwest of Carnegie.

Chapter XII

1. KHRS Kiowa Language folder, Charles and Carrie Redbird (8-4-76).

2. SPC Kickingbird folder (1920) gives Kickingbird's account of his conversion to the Jesus Road years earlier. Also KHRS tape 21 (11-15-78), Linn Pauahty version.

3. Ibid. For some missionary influence see Burnham (1878, 1881), Clouse (1902), Brooke (1903), and Bishop Brooke's correspondence

in the archives of the Church Historical Society: Episcopal
Church, Fort Worth, Texas.

4. Redbird (1962), pp. 1-12.
5. KHRS tape 58 (1976), song by Ioleta Hunt McElhaney Tiger.

Chapter XIII

1. SPC Peyote folder, the account by Monroe Tsatoke (1936) to Susie
   Peters of his exhiliration during a Peyote assembly.
2. Ibid., Maggie Smoky's account entitled "Kiowa Indians on Peyote"
   in which she describes a Kiowa peyote meeting of September 24,
   1920. The Peyote Priest was Charlie Johnson; the Fire Chief was
   Homer Buffalo; the honored person was Old Man Sankadota.
   Twenty-five men and two women (Susie Peters and Maggie
   Smoky) attended.
3. SPC Koy-tah-le (Robert Onco) folder (n.d.) gives the legend of the
   Peyote Women.
4. KHRS tapes 507/565 for the prescribed Peyote ritual by Walter
   Ahhaity, Nelson Big Bow, and Harding Big Bow.
5. KHRS tape 59 (8-14-74), account by James Auchiah and Linn
   Pauahty.
6. Stewart (1974) argues that peyotism preceded, coexisted, and
   survived after the Ghost Dance disappeared. He claims
   disagreement with many scholars, including La Barre (1938, 43),
   Newcomb (1970, 12), and Marriott and Rachlin (1971, 10-21), who
   seemingly suggest that peyotism as a general movement arose after
   the demise of the Feather Dance. The KHRS agrees with Stewart in
   his thesis that peyotism preceded and outlasted their Feather
   Dance.
7. SPC Peyote folder, Susie Peters' account (n.d.) suggests a later
   beginning in accordance with some of her informants.
8. KHRS tape 593, account by Linn Pauahty (1970); this informant
   has recorded 311 "Songs of the Mescal Rite," some with
   "vocables" and some with "words."
9. Moses (1978) discusses James Mooney's role in the peyote
   controversy.
10. Philip (1973) covers the effort of John Collier to support cultural
    freedom and peyote usage by the Native Americans.
11. KHRS account by author of a 1978 Peyote worship near Lawton,
    Oklahoma.
12. KHRS tape 507, account by Walter Ahhaity, Nelson and Harding
    Big Bow (n.d.).
13. SPC Peyote Religion folder, meeting of May 26, 1923, at I-see-o's
    home near Fort Sill. Chief Priest was Old Man Horse; Fire Chief

was Freeman Cat. Forty-two men and ten women were present. Instead of a Water Woman, Maxey Frizzelhead brought the water.

14. Ibid., Monroe Tsatoke's prayer (1935).

15. Ibid., part of Monroe Tsatoke's explanation. Some of Tsatoke's experiences were recorded in *The Peyote Ritual: Visions and Descriptions of Monroe Tsa-toke* by Leslie Van Ness Denman (San Francisco, 1957).

16. Ibid.

17. Ibid.

18. Ibid.; also KHRS Ceremonial Dance folder 2, Pauahty interview (12-18-80).

19. Ibid.

20. Ibid.

21. Mooney (1891).

22. KHRS History folder, James Auchiah (9-8-74).

23. SPC Peyote Religion folder, Monroe Tsatoke (1935).

24. Ibid.

25. Ibid., Susie Peters' account (1937).

26. Ibid.

27. Ibid.

28. KHRS Kiowa Peyote Songs, including those of Tsatoke's, are sung on tapes 547-549 by Ralph Turtle, Nathan Doyebi, Edgar Goulhaddle, James Aunquoe, Emmett Williams, Ernest Redbird, Edward Hummingbird, Oscar Tahlo, Allen Tsonetokoy, and Francis Tsonetokoy.

29. SPC Kiowa Lore folder 6, contains the statement that a descendant of Lone Wolf supplied this information about the bird-tail and the "keeper of the bird" in 1920.

30. SPC Peyote Religion folder, Susie Peters account (1937).

31. KHRS tape 565, Nelson and Harding Big Bow on "Peyote Ritual."

Chapter XIV

1. KHRS History folder, Auchiah account (9-8-74).

2. Ibid. The Kiowa Gourd Clan is actually a society continuing the traditions of an old warrior's society of the horse-buffalo culture days.

3. Ibid.

4. KHRS tape 4, Mark Sadongei (7-3-76).

5. KHRS tape 6, society report (3-4-76).

6. Ibid.

7. KHRS tape 43 (7-14-74), Pauahty account.

8. Ibid.

9. KHRS tape 6, society report (3-4-76).

10. SPC Satanta folder, James Auchiah account (1929).
11. KHRS Ceremonial Dance folder 2, Pauahty interview (12-18-80).
12. Ibid.
13. KHRS tape 301; Oscar Tahlo, Leonard Cozad, and Jasper Sankadota sing the "Farewell Song."
14. KHRS History folder, James Auchiah (9-8-74).
15. Ibid.; also Linn Pauahty (12-18-80).
16. KHRS tape 301; Oscar Tahlo, Leonard Cozad, and Jasper Sankedota; also KHRS tape 43; Pauahty (7-14-74).
17. Ibid.
18. KHRS tape 43, Pauahty (7-14-74).
19. Booklet entitled *Kiowa Gourd Clan Ceremonials*, July 1-4, 1976, p. 14.
20. Smithsonian Institution: Bureau of American Ethnology, Photograph Collection, two nineteenth-century Kiowa skin paintings depicting the Sun Dance ceremonial and the "Brush Dance."
21. KHRS Ceremonial Dance folder 2, Pauahty (4-3-76).
22. KHRS tape 11, Edna Hokeah and Linn Pauahty (2-19-72).
23. Ibid.
24. Ibid.

Chapter XV

1. SPC Prayers and Poems folder, Susan Peters' account (n.d.).
2. Ibid.
3. KHRS Ceremonial Dance folder, Roland Whitehorse (6-10-76).
4. Ibid., Pauahty (4-3-76).
5. KHRS tape 354 (n.d.), '49 Dance Songs by Yale and Ruth Spottedbird, Nathan Doyebi and James Aunquoe; also KHRS tape 43, Pauahty (7-14-74).
6. Ibid.; the general works in the area of Native American music are Laubin (1977) and Highwater (1977); Rhodes (n.d.) has introduced Kiowa music in his work.
7. KHRS tape 43, Linn Pauahty interview (7-14-74).
8. Ibid.
9. KHRS tape 267, Circle Dance and Song by Melvin Gieonty and K. E. Edwards; also tape 354 for '49 Dance Song by Yale and Ruth Spottedbird.
10. KHRS tape 354, song by Nathan Doyebi and James Aunquoe.
11. KHRS tape 278, song by Leonard Cozad, Oscar and Laura Tahlo, and Jasper Sankadota.
12. KHRS tape 43, Pauahty interview (7-14-74).

Bibliography

PRIMARY SOURCES

Manuscript and Taped Sources: Kiowa Oral History

The Kiowa Historical and Research Society (KHRS) has supplied material on tapes and written information in folders which includes the society's consensus or personal interviews on specific subjects. The society headquarters is at Chieftain Park, Carnegie, Oklahoma. A copy of their material used in this study will be deposited in the Manuscripts Collection of Texas Christian University.

Kiowa Historical and Research Society: Oral Interviews (KHRS folders)

FOLDER	SUBJECT	SOURCE
KHRS Medicine folder	Buffalo Medicine	Ta-ne-haddle and Linn Pauahty
KHRS History folder	Kiowa history during horse-buffalo culture days	James Auchiah
Sun Dance folder	Tai-may, Medicine Wheel, Sun Dance	Jacob Ahtone George Tahbone Linn Pauahty
Kiowa Language folder	Language complexity and old and new spelling	Charles Redbird
Ceremonial Dance folder #1	Sun Dance Buffalo (War) Dance Ohoma Dance Buffalo Medicine Cult Dance	Guy Quoetone Linn Pauahty Lee Satepetaw
Ceremonial Dance folder #2	Gourd Dance Feather Dance	KHRS consensus
Ceremonial Dance folder #3	Scalp Dance Warrior's Dance Black Legs Dance	Linn Pauahty
Ceremonial Dance folder #4	Rabbit Dance Death Songs Travel Songs Wind Songs	KHRS consensus

Kiowa Historical and Research Society (KHRS): Oral History

KHRS TAPE NUMBER	SUBJECT	INFORMANTS
1 (4-11-1970)	Kiowa origins, migration, legends, early art, buffalo hunts	Guy Quetone James Auchiah Ioleta Hunt McElhaney
3 (1-10-1971)	Origins, life in the	Re-recording of 1926

		Yellowstone, dwellings, pre-horse culture, migrations	accounts: Hummingbird Blue Jay, or Togemat Tah-poodle, or Humpy Brave Bear Odle-paugh (son of Satank) Kickingbird
4	(7-3-76)	Kiowa life during transition, 1868-1890	Mark Sadongei
6	(3-4-76)	Kiowa War Chiefs of Old Dancing Societies	KHRS consensus report
11	(2-19-72)	Family patterns	Edna Hokeah Pauahty Linn Pauahty
12	(4-22-72)	Kiowa family patterns Medicine priests Spoken word of law Woman's war story	James Auchiah Guy Quoetone James Twohatchett Carole Frame Roland Whitehorse Edna Hokeah Pauahty Linn Pauahty Gillett Griswold Allen Tsonetokoy
21	(11-15-78)	Relations with tribes, Kiowa origins, early culture, migrations, Kiowa calendars, Sun Dance, Kiowa bands, Rabbit Dance, coming of white men	Gina Quoe-tone Pauahty Linn Pauahty
22	(12-17-75)	Kiowa marriage customs, social ethics, social ranks of families, Kiowa captives, custom of naming people	Margaret Hunt Tsoodle
31	(4-3-71)	Kiowa food meat, fruits	Laura Whitehorse Carole Frame Ioleta Hunt McElhaney Parker McKenzie James Auchiah Roland Whitehorse Guy Quoetone Gillett Griswold Linn Pauahty
33	(4-4-76)	Kiowa stories and legends: Chiefs Big Meat, Sankadota, I-see-o, Frizzlehead	David Apekaume

41	(7-12-75)	Genesis of Kiowa people	KHRS consensus report
42	(8-14-74)	Kiowa tipis	Duke Tsoodle James Twohatchett James Auchiah Parker McKenzie
43	(7-14-74)	Kiowa music, dance, song	Linn Pauahty
44	(2-12-76)	Transition years 1867-1890, cattle and farming	Ernest Hunt
45	(5-10-75)	Kiowa stories and legends: buffalo head skull, Chief Stumbling Bear, Chief Lone Wolf	David Apekaume
46	(4-2-76)	Sayn-day stories, Sayn-pete stories, the alligator story	Lee Satepetaw
47	(7-2-76)	Kiowa stories and legends: famine story, Ah-tah-skon- mah and the buffalo medicine, Boy-God (Tah'-lee) legend	David Apekaume
48	(4-4-76)	Kiowa stories and legends: Chief Daring Wolf, woman sacrificed her husband, penalty paid	David Apekaume
51	(12-12-75)	Kiowa reservation life, early teacher education and school life, missionary activity among Kiowa	Ioleta Hunt McElhaney
53	(7-17-75)	The Greats and the Spirit Forces, Kiowa mythic origins	KHRS consensus report
54	(8-14-74)	Kiowa tipis	Duke Tsoodle James Twohatchett Parker McKenzie
55	(4-20-75)	Memorial ceremony for James Auchiah	Guy Quoetone Linn Pauahty
56	(11-20-74)	Sayn-day stories	Eilene Bointy Queton
57	(2-5-76)	Kiowa legends: the Star Girls legend, the "Pulling-out" band.	Jimmie Quoetone
58	(no date)	Sayn-day legends, stories and legends of Kiowa chiefs	Ioleta Hunt McElhaney
59	(8-14-74)	Kiowa culture during	James Auchiah

| | horse-buffalo days | Parker McKenzie
Linn Pauahty |
| 60   (10-14-76) | Kiowa legends | Eva Setapauhoodle |

Kiowa Historical and Research Society (KHRS): Kiowa Dance and Song

KHRS TAPE NUMBER	SONGS	DRUMMERS-SINGERS
101	Gomda Dawgyah (Wind Songs)	Sallie Hokeah Bointy
131/137	Warrior's Dance	Nathan Doyebi, James Aunquoe Ruth and Ernest Redbird
140	Ohoma Dance	Leonard Cozad, Gus Palmer Jasper Sankadota
140-A	Ohoma Dance	Kiowa Ohoma Singers
265	Kiowa Veterans Honors Songs Kiowa Flag Song Thunderbird War Song	Kiowa Tribal Singers
266	Harvest Dance Oklahoma Two Step	Kiowa Tribal Singers
267	Circle Dance Oklahoma Two Step	Melvin Gieonty, K. D. Edwards
274	Circle Dance Oklahoma Two Step	Nathan Doyebi, James Aunquoe Ruth and Ernest Redbird
278	Circle Dance Oklahoma Two Step	Leonard Cozad, J. Sankadota Oscar and Laura Tahlo
301	Tiah-Pah Society (Warrior's)	Oscar and Laura Tahlo Leonard Cozad Jasper Sankadota
305	Black Legs Society (Warrior's)	Leonard Cozad Oscar and Laura Tahlo Jasper Sankadota
354	'49 Dance Songs	Yale Spottedbird Ruth Spottedbird Nathan Doyebi, James Aunquoe
507/565	Peyote Ritual	Nelson and Harding Big Bow Walter Ahhaity
547	Kiowa Native American Church songs	Ralph Turtle, Nathan Doyebi Edgar Gouladdle James Aunquoe

548	Kiowa Peyote Songs	Emmett Williams Nelson Big Bow Edgar Gouladdle Nathan Doyebi
549	Kiowa Peyote Songs	Ernest Redbird Nelson Big Bow James Aunquoe
560/580	Kiowa Peyote Songs	James Aunquoe, Oscar Tahlo Ernest Redbird Allen Tsonetokoy Francis Tsonetokoy
590	Kiowa Peyote Songs	Edward Hummingbird
591	Kiowa Peyote Songs	Nelson Big Bow
592	Kiowa Peyote Songs	Edgar Gouladdle
593	Kiowa Peyote Ritual Songs	Linn Pauahty & Others

The Susan Peters Collection (hereafter referred to as SPC)

The Susan Peters Collection (SPC) includes individual statements by many Kiowas, newspaper and magazine clippings, personal interviews, memoirs, and death-bed accounts collected by Susie Peters from many Kiowas between 1918 and 1963. Many of the records were handwritten and some were typed on paper which included such diverse forms as napkins and envelopes, tablets and bond typing sheets. Stored by Susie Peters in numerous cardboard boxes while she served as Field Matron to the Kiowas, the material required transcription and classification. The basic accounts are included in the second volume of *Kiowa Voices: Myths, Legends and Folk Tales*. The limited use of the collection for this volume came from the following folders.

SPC FOLDER	PRIMARY CONTENT
Kiowa Lore #1	James Auchiah papers on Kiowa dancing orders, Satanta, family traditions.
Kiowa Lore #2	Kiowa migration, the Lost Band account
Kiowa Lore #3	T'ebodel account (1919) on Sarsis, Dohasan, wagon and migration from Black Hills
Kiowa Lore #4	Big Tree's account of Kiowa history; his calendar
Kiowa Lore #5	Satank's Medicine Arrow traditions, war path accounts, miscellaneous
Kiowa Lore #6	Indian lore about Rabbits, Herders, and six dancing societies
Kiowa Lore #8	Kiowa medicine men and Buffalo Medicine Cult traditions
Yellow Wolf's folder (1920)	The memoirs and legends about and by Yellow Wolf; family history
Charley Buffalo's folder (1943)	Legend of the Buffalo Woman, Kiowa legends of the war path, Poor Buffalo and Koitsenko traditions

Peyote (Kiowa) folder (1935-37)	Personalized accounts of Peyote meetings and art designs drawn from worship by Monroe Tsatoke
Artists (Kiowa) folder	Information by Susan Peters on the "Five Kiowa" artists; interview in 1936 with A-mai-ah, keeper of the Tai-may
Kickingbird	Kiowa lore and legends told by Kickingbird II as relayed to him by his elder namesake
Battle of the Washita folder	The story of the Battle of the Washita and results from the Kiowa perspective
Prayer and Poems folder	Kiowa prayers, poems, songs and miscellaneous information
Kiowa Captives folder	George Mopope account in 1919 about Kiowa captives, their stories and treatment and life with the tribe
Satanta's folder	Susan Peters and James Auchiah's accounts about Satanta, with miscellaneous information
Palo Duro Canyon folder	The Battle of Palo Duro Canyon and Col. Ranald McKenzie's attack from the perspective of a Kiowa survivor, Maggie Smoky, the wife of Enoch Smoky
Koy-tah-le folder	Miscellaneous papers from Robert Onco, the son of Anko the Kiowa calendar artist

Carole Frame Papers: Accounts by Robert Onco, son of Anko

Fifteen Saynday stories
Feather information
Sunlight Maiden poem
Poetry and Kiowa symbolism

Archival Sources

Anadarko Agency, Anadarko, Oklahoma.
  Allotment files.
Church Historical Society: Episcopal Church, Fort Worth, Texas.
  Bishop Brooke's correspondence.
Fort Sill Museum, U.S. Army, Fort Sill, Oklahoma.
  James Auchiah papers.
  Photographic records.
Museum of the American Indian, Heye Foundation, New York, N.Y.
  Indians' paintings.
Oklahoma Historical Society, Oklahoma City.
  Indian Archives
    Indian warfare
  Kiowa — census, Indian houses, Indian prisoners of war, Kiowa school, military relations, Police.
  Museum — Indian drawings.
  Photographs — Collection.

Philbrook Art Center.
  Kiowa painting.

Smithsonian Institution: Bureau of American Ethnology Collection.
  Indian drawings.
  Manuscript field notebooks of James Mooney.
  Photograph and negative collections.

United States National Archives and Records Service, Office of Indian Affairs.
  Indian drawings.
  Indian photographic collection

University of Oklahoma Library.
  Doris Duke Oral History Collection — Kiowa
  Photographic Collection

University of Oklahoma Museum of Art
  Kiowa Art.

Published Sources

Battey, Thomas C.
  1876.   *Life and Adventures of a Quaker Among the Indians*. Boston.

Berlandier, Jean Louis.
  1969.   *The Indians of Texas in 1830*. Ed. John C. Ewers. Washington.

Brooke, Rt. Rev. Francis Key.
  1903.   Ten Years of Church Life in Oklahoma and Indian Territory, *SM*, Vol. LXVIII, No. 5.

Burnham, Mary D.
  1878.   First-fruits of the Kiowas, Comanches, and Cheyennes, *Churchman*, Vol. XXXVIII, No. 18.
  1881.   Notes of Our Indian Territory Mission, *GMCJ*, Vol. IV, No. 69.

Catlin, George
  1841.   *Letters and Notes of the Manners, Customs, and Condition of the North American Indians*. 2 vols. London.

Clouse, Rev. H. H.
  1902.   Rainy Mountain Kiowa Mission, *Baptist Home Mission Monthly*, Vol. XXIV, No. 7.

Ewers, John C.
  1978.   *Murals in the Round: Painted Tipis of the Kiowa and Kiowa-Apache Indians*. Smithsonian Institution.

Jones, Douglas C.
  1966.   *The Treaty of Medicine Lodge: The Story of the Great Treaty Council as Told by Eyewitnesses*. Norman.

Marriott, Alice.
  1945.   *The Ten Grandmothers*. Norman.
  1963.   *Saynday's People*. Lincoln.

Methvin, Rev. J. J.

1927.   *Andele, or the Mexican Kiowa Captive.* Anadarko.

Mooney, James.

1896.   *The Ghost Dance Religion and the Sioux Outbreak of 1890,* Bureau of American Ethnology, Fourteenth Annual Report, Pt. 2. Washington.

1898.   *Calendar History of the Kiowa Indians,* Bureau of American Ethnology, Seventeenth Annual Report, Part 1. Washington.

Nye, Wilbur Sturtevant.

1962.   *Bad Medicine and Good; Tales of the Kiowas.* Norman.

Parsons, Elsie Clews.

1929.   *Kiowa Tales.* New York.

Stuart, Lt. J. E. B.

1957.   The Kiowa and Comanche Campaign of 1860 as Recorded in the Personal Diary of Lt. J. E. B. Stuart. Ed. by W. Stitt Robinson. *The Kansas Historical Quarterly,* Vol. XXIII.

Tatum, Lawrie.

1899.   *Our Red Brothers and the Peace Policy of President Ulysses S. Grant.* Philadelphia.

Taylor, Alfred A.

1924.   Medicine Lodge Peace Council, *Chronicles of Oklahoma,* Vol. II, No. 2.

SECONDARY SOURCES

Bauer, George W.

1979.   Symbolism of the Plains Indians' Sun Dance. *Canadian Geographic,* Vol. 98 (3).

Benedict, Ruth Fulton.

1924.   The Concept of the Guardian Spirit in North America. *American Anthropological Association,* Memoir 29. Menasha.

Brown, Dee.

1970.   *Bury My Heart at Wounded Knee.* New York.

Brown, Joseph Epes.

1953.   *The Sacred Pipe of the Oglala Sioux.* Norman.

Campbell, Thomas N.

1958.   Origin of the Mescal Bean Cult. *American Anthropologist,* Vol. 60.

Curtis, Natalie.

1968.   *The Indians' Book: Songs and Legends of the American Indians.* New York.

Dixon, Joseph K.

1914.   *The Vanishing Race.* New York.

Dunn, Dorothy.

1968.   *American Indian Painting of the Southwest and Plains Area.* Norman.

1969.   *1877: Plains Indian Sketch Books of Zo-tum & Howling Wolf.* Flagstaff.

Eddy, John A.

1974.   Astronomical Alignment of the Big Horn Medicine Wheel. *Science,* Vol. 184, No. 4141, pp. 1035-1043.

Ellison, Rosemary.
    1972.   *Contemporary Southern Plains Indian Painting.* Oklahoma Indian Arts and Crafts
        Cooperative. Anadarko.

Ewers, John C.
    1939.   *Plains Indian Painting.* Palo Alto.
    1968.   Plains Indian Painting. The History and Development of an American Indian Art Form.
        The American West.

Gamble, John I.
    1951.   Changing Patterns in Kiowa Indian Dances. *Acculturation in the Americas, Proceedings
        of the 29th International Congress of Americanists.* Vol. II.

Haines, Francis.
    1976.   *The Plains Indians: Their Origins, Migrations, and Cultural Development.* New York.

Halloran, Art.
    1975.   Kiowa Symbolism in *Oklahoma Today* (Summer 1975).

Harrington, John P.
    1910.   On Phonetic and Lexic Resemblances between Kiowan and Tanoan, *American
        Anthropologist,* Vol. 12.
    1928.   Vocabulary of the Kiowa Language. *Bureau of American Ethnology,* Bulletin 84.
        Washington.
    1940.   Southern Peripheral Athapaskan Origins, *Essays in Historical Anthropology of North
        America.* Smithsonian Miscellaneous Collections, Vol. C.

Highwater, Jamake.
    1976.   *Song From The Earth: American Indian Painting.* New York.
    1977.   *Ritual of the Wind: North American Indian Ceremonies, Music, and Dance.* New York.

Hodge, Frederick Webb (ed.).
    1907.   *Handbook of American Indians North of Mexico.* Bureau of American Ethnology,
        Bulletin 30. Vol. I. Washington.
    1912.   *Handbook of American Indians North of Mexico.* Bureau of American Ethnology,
        Bulletin 30. Vol. II. Washington.

Hoijer, Harry.
    1938.   The Southern Athapascan Languages, *American Anthropologist,* Vol. XL, No. 1.

La Barre, Weston.
    1938.   *The Peyote Cult.* Yale University Publications in Anthropology, No. 19.

Laubin, Reginald and Gladys.
    1977.   *Indian Dances of North America; Their Importance to Indian Life.* Norman.

Leckie, William H.
    1963.   *The Military Conquest of the Southern Plains.* Norman.

Lowie, Robert H.
    1916.   Societies of the Kiowa, *American Museum of Natural History, Anthropological Papers,*
        Vol. XI, Pt. 11, New York.
    1923.   A Note on Kiowa Kinship Terms and Usage, *American Anthropologist,* Vol. XXV, No. 2.

Marriott, Alice L.
    1945.   *The Ten Grandmothers.* Norman.

1968.   *Kiowa Years: A Study in Culture Impact.* New York.

Marriott, Alice and Carol Rachlin.

1971.   *Peyote.* New York.

Mayhall, Mildred P.

1962.   *The Kiowas.* Norman.

McKenzie, Parker, and John P. Harrington.

1948.   Popular Account of the Kiowa Indian Language. *Monographs of the School of American Research,* Albuquerque.

Miller, Wick R.

1959.   A Note on Kiowa Linguistic Affiliations. *American Anthropologist,* Vol. LXI.

Mishkin, Bernard.

1940.   *Rank and Warfare among the Plains Indians.* American Ethnological Society, *Monograph No. 3.* New York.

Momaday, N. Scott.

1969.   *The Way to Rainy Mountain.* Albuquerque.

1976.   *The Gourd Dancer.* New York.

Moses, L. G.

1978.   James Mooney and the Peyote Controversy. *Chronicles of Oklahoma,* Vol. 56 (2).

National Geographic Society.

1974.   *The World of the American Indian.* Washington.

Newcomb, W. W., Jr.

1961.   *The Indians of Texas.* Austin.

Nye, Wilbur S.

1937.   *Carbine and Lance: The Story of Old Fort Sill.* Norman.

1968.   *Plains Indians Raiders: The Final Phases of Warfare from the Arkansas to the Red River.* Norman.

Oklahoma Indian Arts and Crafts Cooperative.

1973.   *Painted Tipis by Contemporary Plains Indian Artists.* Anadarko.

Petersen, Karen Daniels.

1971.   *Plains Indian Art From Fort Marion.* Norman.

Philp, Kenneth.

1973.   John Collier and the Crusade to Protect Indian Religious Freedom, 1920-1926. *Journal of Ethnic Studies, I (1).*

Redbird, Charles and Carrie.

1962.   *Kawy-dawkhyah Dawgyah: Kiowa Christian Songs.* Norman.

Rhodes, Willard.

No date. *Music of the American Indian — Kiowa.* Bureau of Indian Affairs, the U.S. Department of the Interior. Lawrence, Kansas.

Richardson, Jane.

1940.   Law and Status among the Kiowa Indians. *American Ethnological Society, Monograph No. 1.* New York.

Rister, Carl Coke.

1926. The Significance of the Jacksboro Indian Affair of 1871. *The Southwestern Historical Quarterly,* Vol. XXIX, No. 3.

Roe, Frank Gilbert.
1955. *The Indian and the Horse.* Norman.

Sandoz, Mari.
1954. *The Buffalo Hunters.* New York.
1961. *Love Song to the Plains.* New York.

Scott, Hugh Lenox.
1911. Notes on the Kado, or Sun Dance of the Kiowa. *American Anthropologist,* Vol. XIII, No. 3.

Schultes, Richard Evans.
1937. Peyote and the American Indian. *Nature Magazine,* Vol. XXX, No. 3.

Slotkin, J. S.
1956. *The Peyote Religion, a Study in Indian-White Relations.* Glencoe.

Southern Plains Indian Museum and Crafts Center.
1975. *Paintings by Stephen Mopope.* Anadarko.

Spier, Leslie.
1921. Notes on the Kiowa Sun Dance, in Clark Wissler (ed.), *Sun Dance of the Plains Indians.* American Museum of Natural History, Anthropological Papers, Vol. XVI, Pt. 6. New York.
1921. The Sun Dance of the Plains Indians: Its Development and Diffusion, in Clark Wissler (ed.), *Sun Dance of the Plains Indians.* American Museum of Natural History, Anthropological Papers, Vol. XVI, Part 7. New York.

Stewart, Omer C.
1974. Origin of the Peyote Religion in the United States. *Plains Anthropologist,* Vol. 19 (65).

Strong, William Duncan.
1940. From History to Prehistory in the Northern Great Plains. *Essays in Historical Anthropology of North America,* Smithsonian Miscellaneous Collections, Vol. C. Washington.

Vestal, Paul A., and Richard Evans Schultes.
1939. *The Economic Botany of the Kiowa Indians as It Relates to the History of the Tribe.* Cambridge.

Vestal, Stanley.
1948. *Warpath and Council Fire: The Plains Indians' Struggle for Survival in War and in Diplomacy, 1851-1891.* New York.

Voegelin, C. F., and E. W. Voegelin.
1944. Map of North American Indian Languages. *American Ethnological Society, Publication No. 20.* New York.

West, G. Derek.
1963. The Battle of Adobe Walls (1974). *Panhandle-Plains Historical Review,* XXXVI.

Wharton, Clarence.
1935. *Satanta, the Great Chief of the Kiowas and His People.* Dallas.

Whorf, B. L. and G. L. Trager.

    1937.   The Relationship of Uto-Aztecan and Tanoan. *American Anthropologist*, Vol. XVI, No. 1.

Wright, Muriel.

    1951.   *A Guide to the Indian Tribes of Oklahoma.* Norman.

Index

T

Y

Z

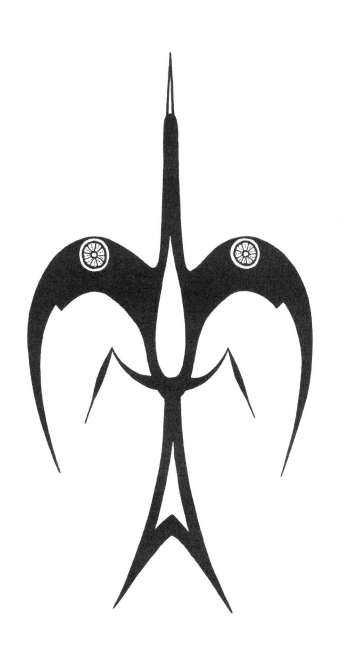

GRAPHIC ART AND DESIGN ARE BY
JUDY OELFKE SMITH.
THE BOOK IS TYPESET IN TEN POINT MELIOR
USING AS DISPLAY TYPE FOTURA BIFORM MEDIUM
BY FORT WORTH LINOTYPING COMPANY,
PRINTED ON 100# PRODUCTOLITH DULL
BY MOTHERAL PRINTING COMPANY
AND BOUND BY JOHN D. ELLIS BINDERY.
COLOR SEPARATIONS ARE BY HARPER HOUSE.